Alive IN THE SPIRIT!

Alive IN THE SPIRIT!

A Study of the Nature and Work of the Holy Spirit

Jimmy Jividen

GOSPEL ADVOCATE CO.
P.O. Box 150
Nashville, TN 37202

Copyright © 1990 by Gospel Advocate Co.

All rights reserved. No part of this publication may be reproduced, stored in a retrieval system, or transmitted in any form or by any means—electronic, mechanical, photocopy, recording, or any other—except for brief quotations in printed reviews, without the prior permission of the publisher.

IT IS ILLEGAL AND UNETHICAL TO DUPLICATE COPYRIGHTED MATERIAL.

Published by the Gospel Advocate Co.
P.O. Box 150, Nashville, TN 37202

ISBN 0-89225-368-1

At the publication of this book I acknowledge my debt to many individuals who have taught me concerning the Holy Spirit. Some of these have been acknowledged in the footnotes. Many others have influenced my thinking in discussions. I have learned from both those with whom I agree and those with whom I disagree in understanding the nature and work of the Holy Spirit.

The basic concepts of two of my tracts, *The Indwelling of the Holy Spirit* and *The Present Work of the Holy Spirit,* are incorporated in this manuscript. Research for two of my books, *Glossolalia* and *Miracles,* was helpful in bringing this book to fruition.

This work would not have been possible without the help and encouragement of those who have corrected errors, offered suggestions and sharpened my focus on many points. I am particularly indebted to Furman Kearley, Edward Myers, Clark Potts, Howard Norton and Don Humphrey, who have made contributions to the finished manuscript in form and content. My extended family, particularly my wife, Shirley, has been my helper and enabler in the total project. It is to them that this book is dedicated.

Jimmy Jividen

FOREWORD

The religious world abounds with confusing and conflicting doctrines concerning the Holy Spirit. Few, if any, doctrines have spawned more divisions in Christendom than the widely varying beliefs concerning the nature and work of the Holy Spirit.

Most of this division and confusion in understanding is because of an ignorance of Scripture, a failure to study carefully all the Bible has to say about the nature and work of the Holy Spirit. Instead, people act out of emotion, follow the doctrines of men and fail to consult the Bible, which is the only source to tell us objectively who the Holy Spirit is and what He does.

Jimmy Jividen, in this book about the Holy Spirit, has done his homework. First of all, he has studied all of the passages that mention the Spirit and examined them in their context. He has explored the key words in the original language so as to obtain the original meaning of the original author to the original audience.

Further, he has studied the scholarly works of a large number and a wide variety of biblical scholars. He has considered the pros and cons of all major views. He has distilled these into clear understandable language.

The final result of his scholarly work is to set forth an excellent summary on the nature and work of the Holy Spirit. He establishes beyond doubt the divine, spiritual and personal nature of the Holy Spirit. This study defines clearly all the important terms and concepts concerning the Holy Spirit.

Foreword

He wades through the confusion and convincingly states the biblical doctrine concerning the baptism of the Holy Spirit, the gift of the Holy Spirit, the different manifestations of the Spirit's power, the indwelling of the Holy Spirit, His work in conversion and His work through the Word of God.

Brother Jividen believes strongly that the Holy Spirit exists, that He has worked throughout history with God and Christ and in behalf of man. He believes deeply that the Holy Spirit is still at work through the Word, through and in the church and also through and in the Christian. He presents the case that the Holy Spirit is very much alive and well, working in spiritual and providential ways for God, for the church and for individual Christians. He proves from the Bible the biblical doctrine concerning the way the Holy Spirit functions in all of these areas.

The reader will receive great benefit by studying carefully this work and reading all of the passages concerning the Holy Spirit. I commend highly this book as a significant help in understanding the truth about the Holy Spirit and recognizing the errors of man's false and divisive theories concerning Him.

F. Furman Kearley, Editor
Gospel Advocate

CONTENTS

FOREWORD iii

INTRODUCTION ix

SECTION ONE
The Nature of the Holy Spirit

ONE: *He Is God* 2
    The Holy Nature of the Holy Spirit 4
    The Spiritual Natural of the Holy Spirit 5
    The Orderly Nature of the Holy Spirit 8
    The Age of the Holy Spirit 10

TWO: *He Is Real* 12
    Idolatry 12
    Religious Experiences 15
    Reality by Faith 18

THREE: *He Is Personal* 20
    Personal Attributes 20
    Personal Action 21
    More than First Cause 21
    The Holy Spirit and the Word of God 23
    The Holy Spirit and Magic 28

SECTION TWO
Understanding Holy Spirit Terms

FOUR: *The Baptism with the Holy Spirit* 31
    Different Interpretations 31
    Scriptural Evidence 32
    It is a Baptism 34
    Two Special Events 37
    The Prophecy of Joel 39

Contents

Pour Forth of My Spirit 42

FIVE: *The Gift of the Holy Spirit* 46
Jesus' Promise of the Holy Spirit 46
Acts 2:38,39 48
The Holy Spirit and the Word of God 52
Points of Confusion 56

SIX: *Measures of the Holy Spirit* 61
Different Works of the Holy Spirit 61
John 3:34 64
Distributions of the Spirit 67

SEVEN: *Indwelling of the Holy Spirit* 72
Old Testament Predictions 73
God Dwells in His Children 75
The Holy Spirit Dwells in the Christian 76
How the Holy Spirit Dwells in a Christian . . . 82

EIGHT: *Spiritual Gifts* 87
Definition 87
Miraculous Spiritual Gifts 88
Purposes of Miraculous Spiritual Gifts 96

NINE: *Blasphemy Against the Holy Spirit* 99
Definitions 99
Three Passages 100
Complementary Passages 103
Conclusions 105

SECTION THREE
The Present Work of the Holy Spirit

TEN: *His Work in Conversion* 112
The Holy Spirit and Conversion 113
Errors About the Holy Spirit in Conversion . . . 116
The Conversion Experience and the Holy Spirit . 117

Alive in the Spirit!
Conversion Influence Beyond the Word 120

ELEVEN: *His Work Through the Word* 124
    The Worker and His Work 127
    Both Spirit and Word 128
    Ephesians 5:18,19 and Colossians 3:16 129

TWELVE: *His Work in the Christian* 136
    Beyond What We Think 137
    Assurance 138
    Moral Help 140
    Providence 142
    Worship 143
    Fruit 144

INTRODUCTION

The motivation for writing this book has come from the author's attempt to bring about balance in the discussion of the Holy Spirit and His work.

On one hand there has been the tendency of some people to think of the Holy Spirit in a subjective, experiential way. This has led to uncritical use of Scripture, unfounded theological speculations and the identification of irrational, emotional experiences with the Holy Spirit. The recent Charismatic movement, though not outwardly affecting many churches, has brought about a change in the thinking of many Christians.

On the other hand there has been the tendency of some people to think of the Holy Spirit in strictly physical, rationalistic terms. This has led to uncritical use of Scripture, unfounded theological speculations and identification of the Word of God along with the work of the Holy Spirit. Although this has not been the dominant view, its advocates have been vocal. There seemed to be a tendency of those who held this view to rely heavily on propositional logic and polemic methods in discussing the Holy Spirit.

It is not the purpose of this author to deny either the place of logic in discovering truth or the place of emotions as an expression of faith. Both have their place. It is the misplacement of logic and emotions that is the root of the misunderstandings of the Holy Spirit.

It is not the purpose of this book to state all of the different theories about the Holy Spirit. This is left to the historian.

Alive in the Spirit!

It is not the purpose of this book to be a polemic against any particular religious party. We hope that the study of this material will help to erase the barriers that exist between parties.

It is not the purpose of this book to give a full discussion of every aspect of the person and work of the Holy Spirit. This would require a document many times the size of the present volume. Other authors have given and will give fuller discussions about many points.

It is not the purpose of this book to arrive at any philosophical certainty concerning the full nature of God, the Spirit, or come to a complete understanding of His work in the world. That would be the height of presumption.

It is the purpose of this book to present, in a balanced and orderly way, what the Scriptures reveal about the Holy Spirit and His work in the world.

SECTION ONE

The Nature of the Holy Spirit

The correct understanding of the Holy Spirit begins with a study of His nature. He exists in a spiritual realm that only can be accepted by faith. All you can know about this realm is revealed in the Scriptures in human terms. To go beyond this is useless theological speculation.

He is God and possesses all of the attributes of God. Human terms may be used to describe His work, but such must not compromise His Godness.

He is real, not just a human emotional feeling. He is the Creator of the universe and man himself. It is folly to think of Him as being created by art and a device of man. It is a form of idolatry to make Him a figment of an emotional experience.

He is personal and relates to man in a personal way. He is not an impersonal force that pervades the universe like the Greek concept of "Fate." He is not a philosophical "First Cause." He can be "grieved" as a person is grieved. He can "groan" to express the yearnings of the Christian's heart before God in prayer.

ONE

He Is God

The first thing to be affirmed about the Holy Spirit is this: "He is God!" He is holy, spiritual, eternal and has all the other attributes of divinity. Much of the misunderstanding about the Holy Spirit would be resolved if His divine nature were understood.

He is not merely a high angel serving God or man. He, like Jesus, was before angels, greater than angels and is worshiped by angels.[1] He is Creator rather than creature. A full understanding of the doctrine of the Holy Spirit was not revealed in the Old Testament; yet, enough is revealed to show the distinction between the Spirit of God and angels.

The Spirit of God was active in the creation process from the very beginning, which is clear in several Old Testament passages.

> And the earth was formless and void, and darkness was over the surface of the deep; and the Spirit of God was moving over the surface of the waters (Genesis 1:2).

> O Lord, how many are Thy works! In wisdom Thou has made them all . . . Thou dost send forth Thy Spirit, they are created; And Thou dost renew the face of the ground (Psalm 104:24,30).[2]

The Spirit of God is not creation, but Creator. That cannot be said of angels. They were a part of God's creation. Like the heavens, the heights, the moon and the stars, angels are to praise Jehovah because "He commanded and they were created" (Psalm 148:5). The Holy Spirit is not merely a high angel.

The Holy Spirit must not be regarded as a neuter force in nature. The grammar of the Scriptures, as well as the theology that is reflected in them, demands that the Holy Spirit be understood as a personal God.

Jesus used the masculine pronoun to refer to the Holy Spirit. The gender of a word does not mean the same in Greek and English. Words that are neuter in English might

---

The first thing to be affirmed about the Holy Spirit is this: "He is God!"

* * * * *

He is not merely a high angel serving God or man. He, like Jesus, was before angels, greater than angels and is worshiped by angels. He is Creator rather than creature.

---

be masculine or feminine in Greek. The word for world, *kosmos*, is neuter in English but masculine in Greek. The word *pneuma*, which is translated "spirit," is neuter; so it usually takes neuter pronouns. That is not always the case when Jesus spoke about the Holy Spirit. He used both the demonstrative pronoun, *ekeinos* (John 14:26; 15:26; 16:8,13,14), and the personal pronoun, *auton* (John 16:7), when promising the Holy Spirit to His disciples. Both are masculine. It is not the Holy Spirit, "It," but the Holy Spirit, "He." "But the Helper, the Holy Spirit, whom the Father will send in My name, He will teach you all things, and bring to your remembrance all that I said to you" (John 14:26).[3] Popular Protestantism, reflecting a back-

He Is God

ground of believing in a "direct operation of the Holy Spirit" in conversion, often still refers to the Holy Spirit as "It"—a double error. The Holy Spirit does not give ecstatic experiences in conversion. He is not to be regarded as an impersonal neuter force.

The Holy Spirit must not be relegated to that body of writings He inspired which is called the Scriptures. (We will discuss this further in Chapters 3 and 11.) This would make Him a neuter force instead of a divine personality. The Holy Spirit who inspired the men who wrote the Scriptures is different from the Scriptures themselves. The Bible teaches that the Word of God is the *sword* of the Spirit (Ephesians 6:17). It does not teach that the Word of God *is* the Holy Spirit Himself. A soldier and his sword are different from each other. One is a person, and the other is the instrument the person uses.

The Holy Nature of the Holy Spirit

The Godness of the Holy Spirit is shown in the way He is referred to in the Scriptures. An understanding of this Godness will, of itself, clear up some misconceptions concerning the Holy Spirit.

The Holy Spirit is, first of all, holy. The word *hagios* signifies an object of awe or reverence. It is the opposite of "profane." The term is used in praise to describe the nature of God. In the temple vision of Isaiah, seraphim praised God: "Holy, Holy, Holy, is the Lord of hosts, the whole earth is full of His glory" (Isaiah 6:3). John recorded the four living creatures in a heavenly scene around the throne of God, praising God: "Holy, Holy, Holy is the Lord God, the Almighty, who was and who is and who is to come" (Revelation 4:8). Holiness is the nature of God. The use of this term with reference to the Spirit reflects the Godness of the Spirit.

Luke, in both his gospel and Acts, connected *hagios* with the Spirit more often than the other New Testament writers. Perhaps this was to distinguish the Holy Spirit

Alive in the Spirit!

from the evil and unclean spirits Jesus confronted in His personal ministry.[4]

The Spiritual Nature of the Holy Spirit

The Holy Spirit is also "spirit" in His very nature. This places Him in the realm of existence differently than physical man. This is shown in the statement Jesus made to His disciples after His resurrection and before His ascension. They were startled when He made an appearance in their midst. He was thought to be a spirit. Jesus corrected their misunderstanding by showing them that His body was physical, and so He could not be a spirit: "See my hands and My feet, that it is I Myself; touch Me and see, for a spirit does not have flesh and bones as you see that I have" (Luke 24:39). A spirit being is non-physical. Spirits exist in a dimension different from the time-bound, physical world. The inability of one's physical senses to perceive the spirit world does not negate the spirit world's existence. All of the accurate information one can know of the spirit world is what is revealed in the Scriptures.

There are both good and bad spirits. They exist in a realm that is not visible. They can relate to man in different ways. The devil is a spirit who can tempt man to sin. God is Spirit and can aid man in overcoming the temptation.

Angels are described as being "ministering spirits" (Hebrews 1:14). God is spirit (John 4:24). Whole orders of angelic spiritual beings exist. They do the bidding of God and surround His throne with praise.[5]

The devil is also a spiritual being. He has angels (Matthew 25:41). There are also fallen angels (2 Peter 2:4). The New Testament speaks of Jesus and the early church confronting evil and unclean spirits during their ministries.[6]

Behind the earthly scenes of the life, death and resurrection of Jesus is a cosmic conflict in the spiritual realm. In the death and resurrection of Jesus, the spiritual forces

He Is God

of darkness were in some way conquered. This is shown in several passages.

The book of Hebrews shows how Jesus' life identified Him with man in the physical realm, and His death conquered the devil in the spiritual realm. "Since the children share in flesh and blood, He Himself likewise also partook of the same, that through death He might render powerless him who had the power of death, that is the devil" (Hebrews 2:14).

It is a false view of the Holy Spirit that expects Him to act in ways contrary to either the laws of nature or the Word of God. The Holy Spirit is not some kind of powerful, playful angel working in whimsical and inconsistent ways. The Holy Spirit is not some kind of errand boy compelled to do the bidding of those who bribe Him with money or manipulate Him with ritual. He is God and by nature is true, consistent and orderly.

Paul showed how Jesus' death on the cross was able to give victory: "When He had disarmed the rulers and authorities, He made a public display of them having triumphed over them through Him" (Colossians 2:15). It was in the spiritual realm that both death and the devil were conquered by Jesus on the cross. The Holy Spirit

Alive in the Spirit!

Himself dwells in this spiritual realm, which Paul described as "heavenly places" (Ephesians 1:3,20; 2:6; 3:10). There is a part of man that is also spirit. Paul described man as possessing body, soul and spirit (See 1 Thessalonians 5:23). Though it is difficult to make clear-cut distinctions within this triune nature of man, it might be understood in this sense:

Man's *body* is the physical part of man that ultimately will go back to the dust of the earth from whence it was created. Man's *soul* is the force by which man lives. In this he has "animal life." He has flesh and blood like the other earth-bound creatures. Man's *spirit* is that part of man that is made in the image of God. It is his real identity. It is that part of man that wills. It is the part of man that never dies.

Paul also divided the inner man into three categories—spirit, mind and heart.[7] Again, it is difficult to make clear-cut distinctions of these divisions in every context, but one is able to understand by observation that they do exist.

The heart seems to involve the feeling part of man—his emotions. The mind seems to involve the thinking part of man—his understanding. The spirit seems to involve the willing part of man—his desire.

It is the spiritual part of man that has communion with God in worship. "God is spirit; and those who worship Him must worship in spirit and truth" (John 4:24).

It is in the spiritual realm that the Holy Spirit helps the Christian in his prayers.

> And in the same way the Spirit also helps our weakness; for we do not know how to pray as we should, but the Spirit Himself intercedes for us with groanings too deep for words; and He who searches the heart knows what the mind of the Spirit is, because He intercedes for the saints according to the will of God (Romans 8:26,27).

Much misunderstanding about the Holy Spirit would be resolved if it were understood that the Holy Spirit is spirit as God is and must not be confined to physical or human attributes. As a spiritual being He is not limited to time and space or subject to physical limitations.

The Greek term translated "spirit" is *pneuma*. It has a broad range of meaning in the New Testament. It can refer to *wind* (John 3:8), *breath* (2 Thessalonians 2:8), *an apparition* (Luke 24:37), *evil and unclean spirits* (Matthew 10:1), *angels* (Hebrews 1:14), *life-principle of man* (1 Corinthians 2:11), *nature of God* (John 4:24), and *the Holy Spirit* (Matthew 1:18).

It is connecting *hagios* to *pneuma* and placing it in the context of divinity that one comes to understand the meaning of the Holy Spirit.

The Orderly Nature of the Holy Spirit

The Godness of the Holy Spirit is shown in that His very nature is truth. Jesus' promise of the Holy Spirit to His apostles emphasized this nature: "But when He, the Spirit of truth, comes, He will guide you into all the truth" (John 16:13).

John's reference to the work of the Holy Spirit in bearing witness to Jesus emphasized this nature: "And it is the Spirit who bears witness, because the Spirit is the truth" (1 John 4:7).

The very nature of God is His truthfulness. It is impossible for God to contradict truth. If God declares a thing to be so, it is so. His creative Word brought the worlds into existence as they are. These worlds and the laws by which they are governed are consistent. His revealed Word declares the plan and promises of the Scriptures as they are. This revelation is true and consistent. Jesus could affirm, "Thy word is truth" (John 17:17).

It is contrary to the very nature of God to contradict truth. Twice in his epistles Paul affirmed this truthful nature of God in order to build confidence in the promises of God. Because it is impossible for God to lie, we can believe His promises and have hope (Titus 1:2; Hebrews 6:18).

Alive in the Spirit!

You can observe the consistency of God in nature. Laws that He spoke into existence at creation are still true. Seeds still bring forth after their own kinds, and the planets still stay in their orbits. God does not act in whimsical ways in nature. He is the God of order and not of chaos.

You can observe the consistency of God in revelation. What God has said, He will do. His commands are authoritative. His promises are sure. He does not change His will to conform to the desires of man. He does not contradict Himself in His revelation. He is the God of truth.

The Holy Spirit, as God, was involved in creation. God, who spoke the worlds into existence in the beginning, still sustains them by the Word of His power (Hebrews 1:3). The Word is true because it is from God.

The Holy Spirit, as God, was involved in the revelation of His will to men: ". . . for no prophecy was ever made by an act of human will, but men moved by the Holy Spirit spoke from God" (2 Peter 1:21). This revelation is true because it is from God. You can believe its testimony because it is accurate. You can yield to its commandments because they are true. You can trust in its promises because they will come to pass. The revelation is true because it is from God.

The very nature of the Holy Spirit is truth. He is consistent and orderly. He does not pervert the laws of nature. He does not contradict the Word of God.

It is a false view of the Holy Spirit that expects Him to act in ways contrary to either the laws of nature or the Word of God. The Holy Spirit is not some kind of powerful, playful angel working in whimsical and inconsistent ways. The Holy Spirit is not some kind of errand boy compelled to do the bidding of those who bribe Him with money or manipulate Him with ritual. He is God and by nature is true, consistent and orderly.

He Is God

The Age of the Holy Spirit

The Old Testament does not reveal much about the person and place of the Holy Spirit in God's plan, just as it does not reveal much about the person and place of Jesus in God's eternal purpose. This does not mean that the eternal word of God and the Holy Spirit of God did not exist and were not actively involved in the divine order of things. They simply were not revealed until God's own good time.

In an illustrative sense, you could say that there were three ages of God's dealing with man. The first was the age of the Father, which existed from the beginning to the birth of Jesus. God the Father was most revealed and most active during this period. The second was the age of the Son, which existed from the birth of Jesus to the coming of the Holy Spirit on the day of Pentecost. Jesus the Son of God was most revealed and most active during this period. The third is the age of the Holy Spirit, which began with the coming of the Holy Spirit on the day of Pentecost and will last until Jesus comes again in judgment. The Holy Spirit of God is most revealed and most active during this period.

This illustration is just that—an illustration. Its purpose is to show that different members of the Godhead were most revealed and most active in dealing with men at different times in history. The Holy Spirit age is the last and final age. In this age God's eternal purpose has been revealed in Jesus Christ, and God's final revelation has been given in the Scriptures.

The Holy Spirit is divine. As God, He is spiritual, eternal, holy and truthful. God the Word was God and did not count being equal with God a thing to be grasped (Philippians 2:6). He became Jesus Christ to save man from his sins. God the Spirit was God and did not count being equal with God a thing to be grasped. He became the Holy Spirit to be a helper and comforter for man.

The Holy Spirit's work in the world does not take away from His divinity any more than Jesus' becoming flesh and blood took away from His divinity.

Alive in the Spirit!

Study Questions

1. Explain the difference between "spiritual" and "physical."
2. Give four attributes of the Holy Spirit that reflect His Godness.
3. What contemporary religious teachings undermine the personal, spiritual nature of the Holy Spirit?
4. How is the age of the Holy Spirit a good illustration to show how God has worked in the world? Show the weakness of such an illustration.
5. How does the godly attribute of "orderliness" correct some misunderstandings about the Holy Spirit?
6. Explain how the Holy Spirit helps in a Christian's prayer.
7. Bring a newspaper clipping to class showing an impersonal view of the Holy Spirit.
8. Memory work: John 14:26.

End Notes

[1]Hebrews 1:4-14 shows the superiority of Jesus over angels because of His divine nature. The Holy Spirit, as divine, also would be superior to angels.

[2]See also Job 26:13; Isaiah 32:15.

[3]See also John 16:13-15.

[4]Luke referred to spirits being "evil" six times (Luke 7:21; 8:2; Acts 19:12,13,15,16) and being "unclean" seven times (Luke 4:36; 8:29; 9:42; 11:29; Acts 5:13,16; 8:7). Mark referred to spirits being "unclean" ten times (Mark 1:23,26,27; 3:11,30; 5:2,8,13; 6:7; 7:25). Matthew spoke of "unclean" spirits only two times (Matthew 10:1; 12:43).

[5]See Edward Myers, *A Study of Angels* (West Monroe: Howard Book House, 1978) for a full discussion about angels.

[6]See Everett Ferguson, *Demonology of the Early Christian World* (New York: The Edwin Mellen Press, 1984) for a full discussion about these spiritual beings.

[7]This is particularly done in the context of worship. Worship must be with the spirit and the understanding (1 Corinthians 14:15). Worship also must be from the heart (Ephesians 5:19).

TWO

He Is Real

The Holy Spirit is real. He is a spiritual being, not a physical form. His existence, like God and Christ, is not dependent upon His being perceived by man. The absence of physical form or the inability of His being known by sense perception does not make Him any less real. Like God and Christ, His existence is accepted by faith. That faith comes from hearing the Word of God (Romans 10:17).

A humanistic view of the Holy Spirit is the popular view, held by religious people of many persuasions. Their understanding of the Holy Spirit does not come from what the Scriptures testify but from what they have emotionally experienced. Their understanding is that the Holy Spirit is real because "they feel it down in their heart." They believe that the Holy Spirit is working in what they claim to be healings, visions, economic success, paranormal happenings and "better-felt-than-told" experiences. The existence and work of the Holy Spirit is made to be dependent upon their own experiences.

Idolatry

The humanization of God is not a new thing. Such was the source of idolatry. Pagans built idols so they could see their gods. They made them look as they wanted them to look. They built temples for their gods to live in. They established oracles so they could hear their gods speak. They used a "bag of tricks" to make them say what they wanted them to say. They set apart priests to exorcize

Alive in the Spirit!

demons, heal the sick and bless their enterprises. They created gods in their own image. They made them do and say exactly what they wanted. Paul described this process:

> For even though they knew God, they did not honor Him as God, or give thanks; but they became futile in their speculations, and their foolish heart was darkened. Professing to be wise, they became fools, and exchanged the glory of the incorruptible God for an image in the form of corruptible man and of birds and four-footed animals and crawling creatures . . . For they exchanged the truth of God for a lie, and worshiped and served the creature rather than the Creator (Romans 1:21-23,25).

The neglect of worshiping the real spiritual God led to the creation of counterfeited physical images that they called gods. They wanted the kind of gods they could see, hear and feel through sense perception.

Pagan priests used the same kind of psychological manipulation, false claims and experiential rituals to convince their followers that their gods were real. This was to their social and economic advantage. The priests were supposed to have special knowledge of the gods and special ways to gain their favor. If one wanted the favor of the gods, he must seek the favor of the priests.

Ecstatic utterances were given by priests and priestesses. They claimed these to be the voice of the god.[1] The Sibilene oracles and the Delphi oracles made use of such automatic ecstatic speech to deceive the people into thinking that such was the voice of the gods. This automatic speech, known in more recent times as "tongue speaking," is merely a human phenomenon. It is known in many world religions, ancient and modern, and sometimes completely outside of the religious context.

Ingenious means were used by priests to satisfy the desires of men to know the god through sense perception and emotional stimulation. Altars were built so a priest could be hidden inside. The hidden priest, pretending to speak in a voice like the gods, would answer the requests of the devotees by audible means.

He Is Real

Emotionally charged ceremonies would be used to excite the feelings of the worshipers. Music, chanting, drama, dancing, incense, candles, bloody sacrifices, exotic rituals and even drugs were used by the priest to produce the desired effect. If one could feel "outside himself," "possessed by a spirit" or achieve a state of ecstasy, then their purpose had been accomplished. The devotee "felt different." He was emotionally moved. His consciousness was altered. In very physical- and sense-perceived ways, the worshiper thought he had come to know the gods.

In such a state of emotional fervor, irrational things would be done and experienced. One might have visions. He might fall into a trance or experience automatic actions in some part of his body. He might become unconscious to pain or feel a sense of physical strength and power. He might perceive himself to have entered a new state of being.

Such pagan practices were attempts to bring a spiritual God down to the physical level of man. These pagans wanted a god they could see and hear. They wanted a physical feeling of their god's presence and favor. They wanted a god they could "turn on" and "turn off" like a television set. This was another form of idolatry. They made gods look like they wanted them to look and do the things they wanted them to do. This was the description of idolatry given by Jeremiah.

> For the customs of the peoples are delusion; Because it is wood cut from the forest, the work of the hands of a craftsman with a cutting tool. They decorate it with silver and gold; They fasten it with nails and with hammers so that it will not totter. Like a scarecrow in a cucumber field are they, and they cannot speak; They must be carried, because they cannot walk (Jeremiah 10:3-5).

It is just as foolish to worship a delusion that comes from the emotions of human experience as it is to worship a delusion that comes from the creation of human skills.

Alive in the Spirit!

Religious Experiences

Much of the misunderstanding of the Holy Spirit could be overcome if it were understood that He is God. He is spiritual; He is personal; He is real and is revealed in the Scriptures. His work is genuine and is according to the Scriptures. If this were understood, His presence would not be confused with the experiences of man.

The emotional feelings of man, even in a religious context, have nothing to do with the being or the work of the Holy Spirit. Such feelings are experienced by Christians, pagans and infidels. They are human feelings and are not to be confused with divine intervention.

Such emotional feelings are unstable and contradictory and must not be used as a criterion of truth or error. Human feelings change with time and are interpreted according to one's own personal inclination or cultural expectancy. Emotional experiences are even understood in different ways by the same individual at different times in his life.

This is demonstrated graphically by the apostle Paul. At one time he sincerely believed he ought to persecute Christians. He consented to their death and believed it

---

The Holy Spirit is a real spiritual personality, not a mere emotional feeling of man. It is a form of idolatry to connect either the figment of one's imagination or the emotional feelings of his heart with the Holy Spirit of God.

---

was the right thing to do. He felt right even when he was doing what was wrong. "Brethren, I have lived my life with a perfectly good conscience before God up to

He Is Real

this day" (Acts 23:1). He thought he was doing the right thing when he held the coats of those who stoned Stephen, but he was wrong. Paul's feeling had nothing to do with the truthfulness of the message he preached or the conduct of his life.

. . . emotional feelings are unstable and contradictory and must not be used as a criterion of truth or error. Human feelings change with time and are interpreted according to one's own personal inclination or cultural expectancy. Emotional experiences are even understood in different ways by the same individual at different times in his life.

God does not sanction "every man's doing what is right in his own eyes." He might believe it is the right thing to do and still be wrong. Human sacrifices have been offered by sincere men who thought they were doing the right thing. Immorality sometimes is practiced by individuals who think it is right. They say, "If it feels so right, how can it be wrong?" There is no right and wrong, good and evil or truth and error if the feelings of men are made the standard.

The wise man in Proverbs affirmed this truth twice, and Jeremiah the prophet made it even more clear: "There is a way which seems right to a man, But its end is the way of death" (Proverbs 14:12; 16:25). "I know, O Lord, that a man's way is not in himself; Nor is it in a man who walks to direct his steps" (Jeremiah 10:23). Depending on the emotional experiences or the human reasonings of

Alive in the Spirit!

man as a criterion for knowing the presence of God or the will of God is folly. It is a form of idolatry.

Experiential feelings change with time and often are contradictory to the feelings of others. How can one know his feelings are right when others who are just as sincere have feelings that contradict? If human emotional experiences are evidence of the Holy Spirit, why cannot the same kind of human emotional experiences also be evidence of the presence and approval of a pagan deity? The feelings are of the same nature.

Human emotional experiences can be wrong. Certainly, they are not a criterion for determining the presence of God or the favor of God; logic prohibits it. The Scriptures themselves express it clearly:

> And for this reason God will send upon them a deluding influence so that they might believe what is false, in order that they all may be judged who did not believe the truth, but took pleasure in wickedness (2 Thessalonians 2:11,12).

The one who believes his human emotional experience is from the Holy Spirit well could be under a delusion. John warns against such delusions: "Beloved, do not believe every spirit, but test the spirits to see whether they are from God; because many false prophets have gone out into the world" (1 John 4:1).

It is possible to believe a lie. This is demonstrated by sincere religious people, who have used an emotional experience, which they believe to be the Holy Spirit, to confirm their faith in a doctrine, a practice or a church. How can the Holy Spirit give confirming approval of individuals who believe different doctrines, practice different rituals and give allegiance to different churches? Something must be wrong. Surely, the Holy Spirit is not the author of confusion.

The Holy Spirit is a real spiritual personality, not a mere emotional feeling of man. It is a form of idolatry to connect either the figment of one's imagination or the emotional feelings of his heart with the Holy Spirit of God.

He Is Real

The existence or presence of the Holy Spirit of God is not determined by one's physical or emotional perception of Him.

Reality by Faith

There is a reality beyond that known by sense perception. It is a reality known by faith. If you believe the God of the Bible and accept His revelation in the Scriptures, you can know this reality. The book of Hebrews reveals how this is done:

> Now faith is the assurance of things hoped for, the conviction of things not seen. For by it the men of old gained approval. By faith we understand that the worlds were prepared by the word of God, so that what is seen was not made out of things which are visible (Hebrews 11:1-3).

Things not visible to sense perception are known by faith. This is how we can understand how the worlds were made.

If the Scriptures had not revealed how the worlds were made, then there would have been no way of knowing, and any theory would be idle speculation. The knowledge of what is not revealed through sense perception can come only from faith. The basis of that faith can be only the word of God.

Knowledge about the Holy Spirit does not come through sense perception. The Holy Spirit has no physical form to see or audible voice to hear. Knowledge about the Holy Spirit does not come through emotional feelings. Such feelings can be deceptive, changing and often contradictory. Knowledge about the Holy Spirit can come only through revelation in the Word of God. We accept His being by faith. We can understand His attributes and know His work only by faith.

Faith that comes from the Word of God sets the limits on who the Holy Spirit is and what He does. We accept all, but not more than, the Scriptures say about Him.

Alive in the Spirit!

Study Questions

1. How is an experiential understanding of the Holy Spirit like idolatry?
2. List four human emotional feelings that some religious people interpret as being from the Holy Spirit.
3. Give two reasons why we should not accept feelings as a criterion for truth and error.
4. Show at least five experiential pagan religious practices that are used in Charismatic religions today.
5. Is a Christian to be void of emotional feelings in his relationship with God? If not, show their place.
6. On what basis can one trust the existence of any reality that is not based on sense perception?
7. Bring a newspaper clipping to class that shows an experiential view of the Holy Spirit.
8. Memory work: 1 John 4:1.

End Note

[1] See Jimmy Jividen, *Glossolalia, From God or Man* (Fort Worth: Star Bible Publications, 1972) for a fuller discussion of the tongue-speaking phenomenon.

THREE

He Is Personal

The correct understanding of the Holy Spirit is often clouded with misconceptions. The source of these misconceptions is sometimes found in men trying to impose the non-biblical thought patterns of Greek philosophy and pagan superstition upon the biblical teaching. Sometimes these misconceptions are the result of trying to support a false doctrine that can survive only through a misconception of the Holy Spirit.

The Holy Spirit is a person in the same way that God and Christ are persons. Just as we relate to God and Christ personally, so also we relate to the Holy Spirit personally, for the Holy Spirit is a personal God.

The Scriptures reveal the Spirit's personal attributes. He can be related to as a person. He acts as a person and responds to man in ways that only a person can. The following charts show Scriptures that express His personality.

Personal Attributes

1. Mind — Romans 8:27
2. Knowledge — 1 Corinthians 2:11
3. Will — 1 Corinthians 12:11
4. Love — Romans 15:30
5. Can be grieved — Ephesians 4:30
6. Can be lied to — Acts 5:3
7. Can be resisted — Acts 7:51
8. Can groan — Romans 8:26

Alive in the Spirit!

Personal Action

1. Speaks	1 Timothy 4:1
2. Testifies	John 15:26
3. Guides	John 16:13
4. Searches	1 Corinthians 2:10
5. Leads	Acts 16:6-7
6. Teaches	John 14:26

The Holy Spirit is not an impersonal force of a mechanical universe that has always existed. Such a view of ultimate reality might fit into the fantasy of "Star Wars" fiction, which dramatized the conflict between the forces of good and evil, but it does not describe the God portrayed in the Scriptures. The work of the Holy Spirit is more than and different from benediction "May the force be with you."

More than First Cause

The non-personal view of the Holy Spirit perhaps had its origin in Greek philosophy. The classical philosophers did not have the benefit of divine revelation in the Scriptures as they sought an explanation of matter and being. They began with the observable world and sought to reason back to the first cause. They saw order in the universe and laws that determined cause and effect. It is not surprising that they, by using only the methods of human reasoning, would postulate the first cause as being an impersonal force.

Aristotle reasoned back to the "unmoved mover" as the first cause. This was not a personal God, but an impersonal force. Plato reasoned back to the "form of the good." Physical reality was only a shadow. The real essence consisted of the impersonal forms that lay beyond the sense—perceived shadows. From Philo of Alexandria to the Stoic philosophers of Greece, the concept of an impersonal permeating force in the universe was a domi-

He Is Personal

nant theme of Greek philosophy. This force was sometimes called *logos*.[1]

It is understandable how one, schooled in Greek philosophical thought and viewing reality as the reasoned conclusions embodied in the "first cause," could identify the Holy Spirit as an impersonal force.

Unaided reason, however important it is, cannot discover God. Such reason might ask the right questions about the necessity of a first cause in the reasoning process and conclude that there is a rational need for God. True knowledge of God, however, can only come from His self-disclosure in the Scriptures and in His incarnation in the person of Jesus Christ. The "proofs for God" as outlined by Anselm and Aquinas, do not prove either the existence of God or the nature of His being. They can only show that such a God is reasonable and fits the order of things.

Paul described the folly of seeking to discover God by reason. In four verses of Scripture, Paul negated Greek philosophy, Jewish scholasticism, and Roman rhetoric as ways of discovering God.

> Where is the wise man? Where is the scribe? Where is the debater of this age? Has not God made foolish the wisdom of the world? For since in the wisdom of God, the world through its wisdom did not come to know God, God was well pleased through the foolishness of the message preached to save those who believe. For indeed Jews ask for a sign, and Greeks search for wisdom; but we preach Christ crucified to Jews a stumbling block, and to Greeks foolishness (1 Corinthians 1:20-23).

Knowledge of a personal God comes through revelations in the Scriptures and in the life of Jesus Christ. The heavens might declare the glory of God and the firmament might show His handiwork, but real knowledge of a personal God cannot be discovered either by nature or Aristotilean logic.

The Holy Spirit is not a glorified, neuter "it." He is a personal God. He must be thought of in the same way

Alive in the Spirit!

as God the Father and God the Son. He is God the Spirit. He cannot be discovered through reason but is known by faith. One believes the testimony of the Scriptures, which reveal both the identity and nature of the Holy Spirit.

It is because of the nonpersonal misconceptions of the Holy Spirit that He often is spoken of as "it." One person might ask, "Have you received it?" and be referring to the Holy Spirit whom he views as a mysterious force. Another might say, "I've got it" and be referring to the Holy Spirit whom he views as an emotional experience. Still another might say, "I received it at baptism" and be referring to salvation, which he believes to be the *gift* of the Holy Spirit.

The Holy Spirit and the Word of God

Sometimes leaders of the church have been accused of depersonalizing the Holy Spirit by equating Him with the Word of God. The charge is made that "the church teaches" that the Holy Spirit is confined to what is contained between the leather covers of the King James Version of the Bible. This charge is similar to what Pat Boone thought about the teachings he received in churches of Christ (*A New Song*, Creation House, Carol Stream, Illinois, 1973):

> You see, I've always been taught that we take the Holy Spirit in us as we read the Word of God, the Bible. The Spirit is in the Word, and as we make the Word of God a part of our daily lives, to that degree the Spirit dwells in us. The Spirit is contained in the Word, and if the Word guides us, then we can truly say that the Spirit is guiding us.

Clearly, this understanding is depersonalizing to the Holy Spirit. And enough people in enough places have made enough similar charges that it should be taken seriously.

Have most leaders of the church of Christ taught a depersonalized view of the Holy Spirit and sought to limit

He Is Personal

His activities only to what He does in and through the Word of God? There are several ways to respond to that question.

First, some leaders of the church in some places and at some times have, no doubt, taught this view of the Holy Spirit. Certainly other, more Scriptural, views also have been taught.

Ashley S. Johnson, in *The Holy Spirit and the Human Mind* (Dallas: Eugene Smith, 1950), writes this of the gift of the Holy Spirit:

> The Holy Spirit enters the heart of the believer because he is a son, because he has obeyed the truth; this harmonizes with the promise of Peter to the thousands of believing Pentecostans that they should receive "the gift of the Holy Spirit" on the conditions of repentance and baptism.
>
> The Holy Spirit in the heart—mind—conscience—of the Christian intercedes for him with persistent and inexpressible interest.

J. W. McGarvey, in his very popular and still used *New Commentary on Acts of Apostles* (Des Moines, Iowa: Eugene S. Smith, 1892), affirms the personal indwelling of the Holy Spirit: "The expression means the Holy Spirit as a gift; and the reference is to that indwelling of the Holy Spirit by which we bring forth the fruits of the Spirit, and without which we are not of Christ."

H. Leo Boles in *The Holy Spirit: His Personality, Nature, Works* (Nashville: Gospel Advocate Company, 1942) also affirms the personal indwelling of the Holy Spirit in the Christian: "From the Scriptures quoted above it is clear that the Holy Spirit was promised to Christians, and that he came and was given to those who obeyed the will of God. It is also clear that he dwells in Christians."

J. D. Thomas, in his book *The Spirit and Spirituality* (Abilene, Texas: Biblical Research Press, 1966), clearly affirms that the indwelling of the Holy Spirit is more than merely the Word of God being received by an individual.

Alive in the Spirit!

This understanding also makes clear the expression in Acts 2:38, "and, ye shall receive the gift of the Holy Spirit." Such is promised to every penitent baptized believer just the same as "the remission of sins" is promised to him. (This gift is neither "the word," nor "eternal life" as some interpreters have held, in which case the Spirit would be the giver rather than the object given.)

These books about the Holy Spirit, popular among members of the churches of Christ, bear testimony that many leaders of the church did affirm the personal in-

The Holy Spirit is not an impersonal force of a mechanical universe that has always existed. Such a view of ultimate reality might fit into the fantasy of "Star Wars" fiction, which dramatized the conflict between the forces of good and evil, but it does not describe the God portrayed in the Scriptures. The work of the Holy Spirit is more than and different from the benediction, "May the force be with you."

dwelling of the Holy Spirit. It is a little presumptuous to say that such a depersonalized view of the Holy Spirit was the standard view.

Perhaps someone can say that such a view was taught in a congregation where he was reared or it was what he understood was being taught in a class discussion. But

He Is Personal

the evidence does not merit making such an absolute, blanket statement about what leaders in churches of Christ have taught about the Holy Spirit.

Our view of the Holy Spirit must not be so experiential and mysterious that we question His consistent, orderly work experienced in the lives of Christians all over the world. The Holy Spirit, like God's work in nature, operates in consistent, orderly ways. The Holy Spirit, like God's response to prayer, operates in ways consistent with the promises of the Scriptures. A denial of the subjectivism of experiential religion is not a denial of the work of the Holy Spirit.

Second, we must understand the context surrounding much of the teaching about the Holy Spirit in this century.

A prominent false teaching about the Holy Spirit in the first half of the 20th century was the Calvinistic doctrine of the "direct operation of the Holy Spirit on the heart of a sinner." This doctrine purported that the Word of God was not sufficient to convict the sinner and produce faith unto salvation. The sinner had to wait for God to work on his heart in a better-felt-than-told way before he could be saved. Calvin believed that there was nothing that the sinner could do until God acted in an experiential "work of grace." He wrote in his *Institutes* thus:

> The same Spirit therefore, who spoke by the mouth of the prophets must of necessity penetrate our hearts to persuade us that what was divinely commanded has been faithfully published.

Another false doctrine that was confronted during this period was the Pentecostal teaching of the work of the Holy Spirit in a "second work of grace." This doctrine claims that the Christian does not receive the Holy Spirit until some time after he has been saved. When he receives it, then he is sanctified.

Both of these false doctrines made the Holy Spirit an experiential feeling that defied reason. Because it is a personal experience, it need not be confined to the teachings of the Scriptures.

Alive in the Spirit!

It would only be natural for those religious leaders who refuted these doctrines to emphasize the orderly work of the Holy Spirit as revealed in Scriptures. Some went so far as to deny any work of the Holy Spirit beyond the Word of God. Perhaps what was happening during this period was not so much the affirmation of a teaching that depersonalized the Holy Spirit by confining His work to the Bible, as it was a failure to affirm positive teachings about the Holy Spirit.

The Holy Spirit must not be depersonalized into an emotional feeling. He is a person with whom we can have a relationship, not an emotional, ecstatic experience. The Holy Spirit must not be made a magical genie who can be manipulated by the secret formula held in the hands of the magic worker. The Holy Spirit is God and is not under the control of man.

Third, we must recognize that *the only* information *we have about the Holy Spirit is from the Word of God.* In that sense we can say that the activity of the Holy Spirit is limited to the Word of God and what it teaches. There is no new revelation beyond the Scriptures. This, however, does not limit the present *work* of the Holy Spirit to only what can be done by the Word of God.

The Word of God cannot make "intercession for the saints" (see Romans 8:26). The Holy Spirit can and does

27

He Is Personal

do this. The view that the Holy Spirit works only and solely through the Word of God just does not fit the Scriptural evidence.

The problem comes when we make claims for the Holy Spirit that are beyond those found in the Scriptures. As Romans 8:26 shows, it is true that the Holy Spirit works beyond the Word of God. The Word, however, reveals all that we can know about what the Holy Spirit does. It is

---

. . . we must recognize that the only information we have about the Holy Spirit is from the Word of God. In that sense we can say that the activity of the Holy Spirit is limited to the Word of God and what it teaches. There is no new revelation beyond the Scriptures. This, however, does not limit the present work *of the Holy Spirit to only what can be done by the Word of God.*

---

presumptuous to make claims for the Holy Spirit that have not been plainly revealed in the Scriptures.

The Holy Spirit and Magic

A perversion of the doctrine of the Holy Spirit is most graphically seen in the way He has been depersonalized by magical claims.

Claiming power from the Holy Spirit, religious leaders offer new revelation, miraculous healings, instant spiritual-

Alive in the Spirit!

ity and the ability to become healthy, wealthy and wise. The power comes *through* the one making the claim. Power, praise and payment to the priest/prophet/preacher are necessary to claim the blessings of the Holy Spirit.

By the power of personality, psychological manipulations, good staging and dramatics, those who are caught up in the emotions of the event think something marvelous has happened to them. They are told that it is the power of the Holy Spirit. They, like the Samaritans and Ephesians, are deceived by the magical arts (see Acts 8:9,10; 19:18,19).

The Holy Spirit must not be depersonalized into an emotional feeling. He is a person with whom we can have a relationship, not an emotional, ecstatic experience. The Holy Spirit must not be made a magical genie who can be manipulated by the secret formula held in the hands of the magic worker. The Holy Spirit is God and is not under the control of men.

Study Questions

1. Name at least five of the personal attributes of the Holy Spirit.
2. Name at least five actions of the Holy Spirit that reflect His being a person.
3. What difference does it make whether one understands the Holy Spirit as an impersonal "it" or as a personal God?
4. Discuss the concepts in Greek philosophy of "the first cause" and "the form of the good" and how they are contrasted with the Holy Spirit.
5. Discuss the relationship of the Holy Spirit to the Word of God.
6. Find a book or tract written by a member of the church that advocates that the Holy Spirit operates only through the Word of God. Find one that advocates that the Holy Spirit personally dwells in a Christian.
7. Bring a newspaper clipping or tract to class that describes the Holy Spirit as "it."
8. Memory work: John 16:13.

End Note

[1]The *logos* of Greek philosophy is not to be confused with the *logos* in the writings of John. The former was an impersonal force, the latter was the eternal Word who became flesh in Jesus Christ.

SECTION TWO

Understanding Holy Spirit Terms

A correct understanding of the Holy Spirit involves defining the terms and phrases used in the Scriptures that are connected with the Holy Spirit and His work. If terms about the Holy Spirit are understood in different ways, then discussion about His work becomes very difficult.

Through the centuries erroneous meanings have been given to terms used in the Scriptures that are associated with the Holy Spirit. This has led to error in both faith and practice.

This section will attempt to bring a scriptural understanding to scriptural terms—scriptural meanings to scriptural words.

If, in the process of doing this, traditional thinking is questioned, so be it. If subjective experiential feelings are shown to be invalid in bringing understanding to the work of the Holy Spirit, let it be. If speculative theological theories are challenged, this work will not have been in vain.

A critical examination of these chapters in the light of the Scriptures will bring about a clearer understanding of both the nature and work of the Holy Spirit.

FOUR

The Baptism with the Holy Spirit

One of the scriptural phrases used with reference to the work of the Holy Spirit is "baptism with the Holy Spirit." This *phrase* must be understood in the scriptural sense in order for us to understand the *work* of the Holy Spirit. The different meanings that have been given to this phrase have resulted in some radically different doctrines and practices.

Different Interpretations

The classical Calvinistic understanding of baptism with the Holy Spirit connects it with salvation. Calvin claims it is an "experience of grace" given by God completely apart from the will of man, which assures him of salvation. It is "better felt than told." There is no support for such a view of the baptism with the Holy Spirit in the Scriptures.

Most Pentecostal churches connect baptism of the Holy Spirit with the "second work of grace" or the believer's sanctification. Evidence of this is sometimes thought to be the experience of "speaking in tongues."

The experiential basis for such understanding of baptism of the Holy Spirit is evident. There is, however, no scriptural basis.

If someone has had an unexplainable emotional experience in a religious context, he might rightly be confused. He does not understand its meaning, nor does he know its source. Someone tells him he has received the miracle of "baptism with the Holy Spirit." Without understanding either the meaning of the scriptural phrase "baptism with the Holy Spirit" or the basis of his own experience, he can be persuaded easily that, indeed, he has been baptized with the Holy Spirit.

Such an explanation is uncritical at best and deceptive at worst. His emotional experience is a common human phenomenon. The biblical baptism of the Holy Spirit was received by only a limited number of people at a limited time in the past and for a very special purpose, which we will discuss later in this chapter.

Baptism of the Holy Spirit has been understood by some people as a one-time, miraculous event, which occurred on the day of Pentecost giving the apostles special powers. The experience of the Gentiles gathered at Cornelius' house is understood as being an exception to the rule (see Acts 10).

Baptism of the Holy Spirit has been understood by some as not only an event on the day of Pentecost, but also involving all others after them who have "called on the name of the Lord." In this sense all Christians receive "baptism of the Holy Spirit."

Baptism of the Holy Spirit has been understood by some as a part of water baptism. When someone is baptized in water, it is also baptism of the Holy Spirit.

A scriptural phrase must be understood as it originally was used by the New Testament writers. It is uncritical to use a scriptural term to mean something it did not mean in its original context. It is also uncritical to use a scriptural phrase in a symbolic sense that is foreign to its New Testament meaning.

The Scriptural Evidence

There are six references to baptism with the Holy Spirit in the New Testament. Three are parallel references in the synoptic gospels.[1] Two have identical wording. The first context is the prediction of John the Baptist about the coming Messiah:

Alive in the Spirit!

John answered and said to them all, "As for me, I baptize you with water; but He who is mightier than I is coming, and I am not fit to untie the thong of His sandals; He Himself will baptize you in the Holy Spirit and fire" (Luke 3:16).

Two references are in Acts. One is the promise to His apostles before His ascension. The other is a statement of Peter before the Jewish brethren at Jerusalem.

In the context of Jesus' talking to His apostles about the kingdom of God and their inquiry about its restoration, Jesus promised baptism with the Holy Spirit:

> And gathering them together, He commanded them not to leave Jerusalem, but to wait for what the Father had promised, "Which," He said, "you have heard from me; for John baptized with water, but you shall be baptized with the Holy Spirit not many days from now" (Acts 1:4,5).

It was to be in Jerusalem. It was to be to the apostles. It was going to be "not many days" before it happened.

In the context of his defending his teaching and baptizing Cornelius and his household, Peter told the Jewish brethren at Jerusalem about baptism with the Holy Spirit at Caesarea:

> And as I began to speak, the Holy Spirit fell upon them just as He did upon us at the beginning. And I remembered the word of the Lord, how He used to say, "John baptized with water, but you shall be baptized with the Holy Spirit." If God therefore gave to them the same gift as He gave to us also after believing in the Lord Jesus Christ, who was I that I could stand in God's way? (Acts 11:15-17. See also 15:8).

A similar statement was made by Peter to the Jewish brethren at Jerusalem to defend his preaching at Cornelius' house: "And God, who knows the heart, bore witness to them, giving them the Holy Spirit, just as He also did to us" (Acts 15:8).

The Baptism with the Holy Spirit

These passages identify what happened at Cornelius' house in Caesarea as being the same as what happened to the apostles at Jerusalem on the day of Pentecost. It ties Jesus' promise to baptize with the Holy Spirit to the apostles on Pentecost together with the promise to Cornelius' household.

Nowhere does it say the apostles were baptized with the Holy Spirit on Pentecost. We can only know it by inference.

First, there was the promise from Jesus that baptism with the Holy Spirit would happen to the apostles at Jerusalem a few days after His ascension. We can always believe a promise from Jesus.

Second, Peter identified what happened at Cornelius' house as being baptism with the Holy Spirit as promised by Jesus. He also identified it as being "that which happened at the beginning." This infers that the events on the day of Pentecost involved baptism with the Holy Spirit.

From the Scriptural evidence we can conclude the following about the baptism with the Holy Spirit:

- It was predicted by John the Baptist and contrasted with his own baptism in water.
- It was promised by Jesus in the context of discussing the kingdom of God.
- It was identified by Peter as being related to the events on the day of Pentecost and at Cornelius' house. What happened at Cornelius' house was the same gift. When the Holy Spirit fell on Cornelius' house, it reminded Peter of the promise that Jesus had made about baptism with the Holy Spirit. This caused him to conclude that God approved of baptizing Gentiles as well as Jews.

It is a Baptism

Baptism with the Holy Spirit is to be understood in the context of other baptisms in the Scriptures. There are seven, each one involving a unique immersion or an overwhelming by something.

Alive in the Spirit!
1. The baptism of Moses under the cloud and in the sea (1 Corinthians 10:2).
2. The baptism of Jesus by John (Matthew 3:13-17).
3. The baptism of repentance by John (Matthew 3:2).
4. The baptism of suffering (Mark 10:39).
5. The baptism of believers (Mark 16:16).
6. The baptism with the Holy Spirit (Acts 1:5).
7. The baptism of fire (Matthew 3:11).

We must understand baptism with the Holy Spirit as it is contrasted with the baptism of repentance preached by John the Baptist. The difference involves two things—the baptizer and the element in which the baptism takes place. John baptized with water. Jesus baptized with the Holy Spirit.[2]

Baptism with the Holy Spirit is distinctly different from both the baptism of John the Baptist and the believer's baptism in several ways.

First, baptism with the Holy Spirit cannot be commanded. It is not something you can do for or by yourself. It is accomplished by a direct act of God without any prescribed conditions on the part of the one being baptized. No one in the Scriptures ever prayed to be baptized with the Holy Spirit.

Second, baptism with the Holy Spirit was administered by Jesus. The apostles could not baptize someone with the Holy Spirit.[3] It cannot be accomplished by the laying on of hands, emotional exercises and fervent prayer. It was promised by Jesus to the apostles and conveyed by Jesus to those He chose.

Third, the baptism with the Holy Spirit has nothing to do with salvation in the Scriptures. Its source was God, and its purpose was inspiration and confirmation.

Fourth, baptism with the Holy Spirit was connected with men being able to speak in foreign languages which they had not learned in the normal way. It involved a miracle which could be tested by objective standards.[4] These tongues were not some sort of ecstatic utterances or emotional feeling. They were discernible languages.

35

The Baptism with the Holy Spirit

It is true that baptism in water is closely connected with the Holy Spirit. One is begotten by the Holy Spirit through the Word to become a child of God (James 1:18; 1 Peter 1:23). One is baptized "in one Spirit" into the body of Christ (1 Corinthians 12:13). One is born of the water and Spirit to become a member of the family of God (John 3:5). One receives the "gift of the Holy Spirit" at baptism (Acts 2:38). In one sense of the word, this can be called a baptism in the Holy Spirit. Paul's description of it certainly shows that the Holy Spirit is involved: "For by one Spirit we were all baptized into one body, whether Jews or Greeks, whether slaves or free, and we were all made to drink of one Spirit" (1 Corinthians 12:13). The preposition translated "by" in English is *"en"* in Greek. It can be translated as "by," "in" or "with." It is the same preposition that is used every time baptism "with the Holy Spirit" is mentioned.[5] When one is baptized in water into the body of Christ, it can also be said that he was baptized *"en"* the Holy Spirit.

This does not mean that water baptism is the same as the technical phrase "baptism with the Holy Spirit" predicted by John and promised by Jesus. There are several ways in which they differ. The following chart shows some of their differences.

Point of Comparison	Baptism with Holy Spirit	Water Baptism
1. Baptizer	Jesus	None specified
2. Those being baptized	Twelve Apostles and Cornelius' household	Any penitent believer
3. Element*	The Holy Spirit	Water
4. Purpose	Confirmation from God	Remission of sins and gift of the Holy Spirit

Alive in the Spirit!

Point of Comparison	Baptism with Holy Spirit	Water Baptism
5. Whose choice	God	Whosoever wills
6. Accompanied by	Miracles	Preaching
7. Prerequisites	None given	Faith and Repentance

*Element might not be a good word for the Holy Spirit. It means here the spiritual reality of the Holy Spirit as water is a physical reality.

Even though water baptism is closely connected with the Holy Spirit, it cannot be understood as "baptism with the Holy Spirit" promised by Jesus.

Two Special Events

Luke does not give an exhaustive account of all that happened at either Jerusalem or Caesarea when men experienced baptism with the Holy Spirit. His language does identify them as being the same thing. What happened at Cornelius' house was "just as He did upon us at the beginning" (Acts 11:15). He plainly said that it was "the same gift He gave to us" (Acts 11:17).

Both events could have included "a noise like a violent, rushing wind," "tongues as of fire," and speaking in foreign languages "as the Spirit was giving them utterance."[6] Luke said these happened at Jerusalem, but he does not include the wind sounds or sight of tongues of fire in recording what happened at Caeserea. It could have happened, and Luke just did not record it. It could have been that the events were basically alike in source and purpose but not alike in every detail. We know, in fact, that the people and places were different.

The basic likenesses of the two events were threefold:

The Baptism with the Holy Spirit

The baptizer was the same—Jesus. This had been predicted by John and promised by Jesus Himself.

That in which they were baptized was the same—the Holy Spirit. The texts say that "they were all filled with the Holy Spirit" and that "the Holy Spirit fell upon them" (Acts 2:4; 11:15).

The purposes for the baptism were the same—inspiration and confirmation. Different people were involved in each event, but the theological purposes of inspiration and confirmation were the same.

The apostles on the day of Pentecost spoke by inspiration. Their speech was "as the Spirit gave them utterance." Those at Cornelius' house spoke by inspiration. Luke described it as "speaking with tongues and exalting God."

Baptism with the Holy Spirit in both instances was a miracle. It was to show God's confirmation of both the men and the message they proclaimed. Peter used those miraculous events the people observed on the day of Pentecost as evidence of Jesus' resurrection: "Therefore having been exalted to the right hand of God, and having received from the Father the promise of the Holy Spirit, He has poured forth this which you both see and hear" (Acts 2:33). The miracles involved in the baptism with the Holy Spirit confirmed the message about the resurrection of Jesus as true.

Peter used the miraculous events, observed by the Jewish brethren who came with him to Caesarea, as evidence to show that God had granted salvation to the Gentiles.

> Surely no one can refuse the water for these to be baptized who have received the Holy Spirit just as we did, can he?
>
> If God therefore gave to them the same gift as He gave to us also after believing in the Lord Jesus Christ, who was I that I could stand in God's way (Acts 10:47; 11:17)?

Alive in the Spirit!

Baptism with the Holy Spirit was a confirming sign to validate Jesus' resurrection and the salvation of the Jews.

The Prophecy of Joel

Peter said that the events on the day of Pentecost involved in the baptism with the Holy Spirit were a fulfillment of the prophecy of Joel. In responding to the speculation that the apostles were acting the way they were because they were full of new wine, Peter said, "For these men are not drunk, as you suppose, for it is only the third hour of the day; but this is what was spoken of through the prophet Joel" (Acts 2:15,16).

A careful reading of this prophecy shows that Joel's prophecy was not just for the day of Pentecost but was for all of the last days.

Some of the prophecy was fulfilled on the day of Pentecost—the beginning of the last days. Peter said as much when he declared, "This is what was spoken of through the prophet Joel." The first part of Joel's prophecy fits what happened on Pentecost and within the early church:

> And it shall be in the last days, God says, that I will pour forth of My Spirit upon all mankind; and your sons and your daughters shall prophesy, and your young men shall see visions, and your old men shall dream dreams; Even upon My bondslaves, both men and women, I will in those days pour forth of My Spirit and they shall prophesy (Acts 2:17,18).

Two times in the passage Joel spoke of God "pouring forth" of His Spirit. Certainly this must have been the basic thought that Peter had in mind in quoting this passage. The prophet Joel had predicted the coming of the Spirit. The miraculous events of Pentecost began the fulfillment of this promise.

Another point of this prophecy was that this outpouring of the Spirit would be "upon all mankind." The apostles and the church in Jerusalem must not have understood

The Baptism with the Holy Spirit

the full import of this at first because it took four miracles to convince Peter that the Gentiles could be saved, even though he knew the promise of the Spirit was for "all mankind."

The coming of the Spirit was for both the old and young, male and female. The coming of the Spirit was manifested in prophecy, visions and dreams. The Spirit's coming would be new revelation from God, and it would involve every category of mankind.

The rest of the story in Acts shows how this took place:
- Peter dreamed dreams (Acts 10:9-16).
- Paul saw visions (Acts 16:9).
- Agabus and others prophesied (Acts 11:8).
- Old men like John received revelation (Revelation 1:1).
- Young men like Timothy were involved in receiving gifts through prophetic utterances (1 Timothy 4:14).
- Women like the four virgin daughters of Philip prophesied (Acts 21:9).

The first part of Joel's prophecy was fulfilled at the beginning of the last days. This was during the time when, through the Holy Spirit, God revealed His will through miraculous dreams, visions and prophecy.

Some of the prophecy was to be fulfilled at the end of the last days—when the great and glorious day of the Lord shall come. Part of Joel's prophecy used apocalyptic language to show what was to take place at the end of the age.

> And I will grant wonders in the sky above, and signs on the earth beneath, blood and fire, and vapor of smoke. The sun shall be turned into darkness, and the moon into blood, before the great and glorious day of the Lord shall come (Acts 2:19,20).

There is no record of such things happening on the day of Pentecost. Similar apocalyptic language is used in Scripture for the consummation of this present age.

Alive in the Spirit!

> But immediately after the tribulation of those days the sun will be darkened, and the moon will not give its light, and the stars will fall from the sky, and the powers of the heavens will be shaken, and then the sign of the Son of Man will appear in the sky, and then all the tribes of the earth will mourn, and they will see the Son of Man coming on the clouds of the sky with power and great glory (Matthew 24:29-31).

Similar language is used at the opening of the sixth seal in Revelation 6:12-17. There are apocalyptic predictions of havoc in the heavens and on earth at the "end time" when the wrath of the Lamb is revealed.

Joel's prophecy was not only about the beginning of the last days, it also involved the end of the last days. It is a mistake to try and fit all of the happenings of Joel's prophecy into only a portion of the span of time involved in the last days.

Some of the prophecy would be fulfilled all during the last days—Joel's statement was "every one who calls on the name of the Lord shall be saved." This promise would be true throughout all the last days.

This same passage is quoted by Paul in writing to the Roman church about the scope of the Gospel being for all men.

> For the Scripture says, Whoever believes in Him will not be disappointed. For there is no distinction between Jews and Greeks; for the same Lord is Lord of all, abounding in riches for all who call upon Him; for whoever will call upon the name of the Lord will be saved (Romans 10:11-13).

Joel's prophecy was for all the last days. It involved apocalyptic language, which must not be taken literally or made to fit into only the first day of Pentecost after Jesus' resurrection.

The Baptism with the Holy Spirit

Pour Forth of My Spirit

Joel's prophecy said that God promised, "I will pour forth of My Spirit upon all mankind" in the last days. Richard Rogers suggests, in *A Study of the Holy Spirit of God* (Lubbock: Richard Rogers, 1968), that the meaning and grammar of "pour forth" demands a one-time, never-to-be-repeated act, which is identified as the baptism with the Holy Spirit.

The word translated "pour forth" or "pour out"[7] is used four times of the Holy Spirit in the New Testament.

It is first used in the quotation from Joel in which God says, "I will pour forth of My Spirit upon all mankind" (Acts 2:17). When this happened on the day of Pentecost, the age of the Holy Spirit began. It is evident that the baptism with the Holy Spirit on the day of Pentecost became a whole new era of how God works in the world. The Holy Spirit began to work in new ways in the world, in Christians and in the church. This working included baptism with the Holy Spirit but must not be limited to it.

It is used the second time in the sermon that Peter preached on Pentecost. The visible, audible, physical things that were observed by the multitude at the "pouring forth" of the Holy Spirit was evidence that Jesus was raised from the dead: "Therefore having been exalted to the right hand of God, and having received from the Father the promise of the Holy Spirit, He has poured forth this which you both see and hear" (Acts 2:33). The promise of the Father certainly included baptism with the Holy Spirit.[8] This was the substance of Jesus' statement to His apostles before His ascension.

> He commanded them not to leave Jerusalem, but to wait for what the Father had promised, Which, He said, you heard of from Me; for John baptized with water, but you shall be baptized with the Holy Spirit not many days from now (Acts 1:4,5).

To suggest that baptism with the Holy Spirit was all that was involved in the "pouring forth" of the Holy Spirit is

Alive in the Spirit!

to set limits not set in the Scriptures. Baptism with the Holy Spirit happened in a specific place—Jerusalem. Baptism with the Holy Spirit happened to certain individuals—the apostles. Baptism with the Holy Spirit happened at a certain time—not many days after Jesus' ascension.[9] The activity of the Holy Spirit in the last days involves more than this. There would be prophecy in the last days by the Holy Spirit. There would be wonders in the last days by the Holy Spirit. The pouring forth of the Holy Spirit included baptism with the Holy Spirit, but how can it be said that this was all that was involved?

The idea that the Holy Spirit was "poured out" is used a third time in Luke's report about the reception of the Holy Spirit by the Gentiles. The same word in the same tense is used by Luke as Peter used on Pentecost. Luke must not have known that the pouring out of the Holy Spirit was a once, not-to-be-repeated event on Pentecost. He reported the event this way: "And all of the circumcised believers who had come with Peter were amazed, because the gift of the Holy Spirit had been poured out upon the Gentiles also" (Acts 10:45). It was not just the benefits of the pouring out of the Holy Spirit that the Gentiles received, it was the gift of the Holy Spirit that was poured out upon them.[10]

The fourth place the Word is used is in one of the latter epistles. It was long after Pentecost and the events surrounding the baptism with the Holy Spirit. In the passage the Holy Spirit is said to have been "poured out upon us richly through Jesus Christ our Savior" (Titus 3:6). The aorist tense is used as in Acts 2:33. If the aorist meant a once-for-all, not-to-be-repeated action when it was used by Peter about the multitude in Jerusalem, how could it mean the same thing to Titus in Crete a generation later?

We must reject the idea that the "pouring forth" of Joel's prophecy is limited to baptism with the Holy Spirit because there is no evidence to prove it. Baptism with the Holy Spirit is one of the things involved in the Holy Spirit's being poured out on all mankind, but that is not all that is involved. The references to baptism with the

The Baptism with the Holy Spirit

Holy Spirit in Acts show that the predictions of Joel and John the Baptist were what took place on the day of Pentecost and at the household of Cornelius. Both language and context show this to be true. These two memorable occasions are the only references that can be identified from the Scriptures as being "baptism with the Holy Spirit." Any theory of baptism with the Holy Spirit involving more than these is mere theological speculation.

Study Questions

1. From your study of the six passages dealing with baptism of the Holy Spirit, answer the following:
   - Who was the first to predict it?
   - Who was to administer it?
   - Who promised it?
   - Where and when was it promised to happen?
   - What miraculous signs accompanied it?
   - Who received it?
   - What was its purpose?
2. Compare baptism of the Holy Spirit with water baptism.
3. How was the prophecy of Joel to be fulfilled in the "last days"?
4. What does the Holy Spirit have to do with water baptism?
5. Explain why one cannot be baptized with the Holy Spirit today.
6. Bring a tract or article to class that connects baptism with the Holy Spirit to conversion or sanctification.
7. Memory work: Acts 1:5.

End Notes

[1]Matthew 3:11; Mark 1:8; Luke 3:16. John 1:33 also refers to the baptism with the Holy Spirit in the witness John bore to Jesus.

[2]Jesus also baptized with water during His personal ministry, but John said the "Coming One" would baptize with the Holy Spirit in contrast with his baptizing in water. See John 4:1-2 and Matthew 3:11.

[3]We must not confuse the reception of the Holy Spirit through the laying on of the apostles' hands with baptism with the Holy Spirit (see Acts 8:14-18). The former was done by the apostles, the latter was done by Jesus. The laying on of the apostles' hands is never identified with baptism with the Holy Spirit in the Scriptures.

[4]For a full discussion of the nature of speaking in tongues, its content and its purposes, see Jimmy Jividen, *Glossolalia, From God or Man* (Fort Worth: Star, 1972).

[5]See Matthew 3:11; Mark 1:8; Luke 3:16; John 1:33; Acts 1:5; 11:16. In

Alive in the Spirit!

this manuscript it is translated "with" as in the New American Standard Bible.

[6]These were the external things which surrounded the apostles on the day of Pentecost as shown in Acts 2:1-4.

[7]The fact that *ekcheo* is future in Acts 2:17 and Peter said that this "pouring out" of the Holy Spirit on Pentecost fulfilled this promise does not make it a one-time, for-all-time fulfillment. The fact that *execheen* is aorist in Acts 2:33 does not mean that the "poured forth" witnessed by the multitude was the totality of the work of the Holy Spirit. The fact that *ekkechutai* is perfect in Acts 10:45 does not mean that the baptism with the Holy Spirit only happened on Pentecost and Cornelius only received the continuing results of it. The fact that *execheen* is aorist in Titus 3:6 does not mean that the Holy Spirit was only poured out on Pentecost. Paul's writing to Titus many years later could speak of the Holy Spirit poured out on Titus as well as those at Pentecost.

[8]The promise of the Father no doubt refers back to the promise that Jesus revealed in John 14:16,26; 15:26; Acts 1:4-5. It involved the baptism of the Holy Spirit. We should not confuse this with the promise of the "gift of the Holy Spirit" in Acts 2:38. The former promise was from the Father—to the apostles—of the baptism with the Holy Spirit. The latter promise was from Peter—to as many as the Lord calls—of the gift of the Holy Spirit.

[9]Luke identified the events at Cornelius' house as being the baptism with the Holy Spirit and as being like that which took place on the day of Pentecost (see Acts 11:15-17; 15:8). This occurrence of the baptism with the Holy Spirit was not specified in the promise Jesus made to the apostles before His ascension in Acts 1:4,5. We can identify it as the baptism with the Holy Spirit because of the statement of Luke.

[10]The "gift of the Holy Spirit" received by Cornelius and his house came before they were saved. They received it before Peter spoke "words . . . by which you will be saved" (Acts 11:14). This "gift of the Holy Spirit" is not to be confused with the "gift of the Holy Spirit" promised at baptism (see Acts 2:38; Galatians 4:6). The purpose of the "gift of the Holy Spirit" at Cornelius' house was to convince the Jews that the Gentiles could be saved. Perhaps the phrase *dorea tou agiou pneumatos* is to be understood as a subjective genitive meaning "a gift *from* the Holy Spirit" instead of a subjective genitive meaning "a gift *of* the Holy Spirit" as in Acts 2:38. Such an understanding would fit Paul's statement that the Spirit distributes "gifts" (see 1 Corinthians 12:7-11).

FIVE

The Gift of the Holy Spirit

The gift of the Holy Spirit, along with the forgiveness of sins, was promised to those who were baptized on the day of Pentecost. There can be no question about this because the language is clear: "And Peter said to them, Repent, and let each of you be baptized in the name of Jesus Christ for the forgiveness of your sins; and you shall receive the gift of the Holy Spirit" (Acts 2:38).

The gift of the Holy Spirit, along with the forgiveness of sins, was not confined to the first-century Jews on the day of Pentecost. The promise was "for you and your children, and for all who are far off, as many as the Lord our God shall call to Himself" (Acts 2:39). This makes the gift of the Holy Spirit a present reality. He is received by someone when he is baptized in the name of Jesus Christ.

Some questions immediately come to mind when this teaching is affirmed.

1. Does the Holy Spirit personally dwell in a Christian?
2. Is the gift of the Holy Spirit the Holy Spirit Himself or a gift He gives?
3. How does the Holy Spirit dwell in a Christian?
4. What effect does the indwelling of the Holy Spirit have upon a Christian?
5. How can a Christian know that the Holy Spirit dwells in him?

Jesus' Promise of the Holy Spirit

Jesus in His personal ministry promised that those who believed on Him would receive the Holy Spirit. He used

Alive in the Spirit!

an Old Testament analogy to make this promise. The Holy Spirit would come like water on a dry and scorched land (Isaiah 44:3; 58:11). The source of the Holy Spirit is God. He will "pour the Spirit out" from on high (Isaiah 32:15; 44:3). It will be without cost and available to all who are thirsty (Isaiah 55:1,2).

> Now on the last day, the great day of the feast, Jesus stood and cried out saying, If any man is thirsty, let him come to Me and drink. He who believes in Me, as the Scripture said, From his innermost being shall flow rivers of living water. But this He spoke of the Spirit, whom those who believed in Him were to receive; for the Spirit was not yet given, because Jesus was not yet glorified (John 7:37-39).

The promise of the Holy Spirit was from Jesus.[1] The promise was to believers and would not be received until Jesus was glorified. The conditions of this promise were met on the day of Pentecost.

Jesus' apostles received a special promise of the Holy Spirit. During the last days of His ministry, He told them that He must go away and that the Helper—the Holy Spirit—would come.

> And I will ask the Father, and He will give you another Helper, that He may be with you forever; that is the Spirit of truth, whom the world cannot receive, because it does not behold Him or know Him, but you know Him because He abides with you, and will be in you. I will not leave you as orphans (John 14:16-18).

> But the Helper, the Holy Spirit, whom the Father will send in My name, He will teach you all things, and bring to your remembrance all that I said to you (John 14:26).

> When the Helper comes, whom I will send to you from the Father, that is the Spirit of truth, who proceeds from the Father, He will bear witness of Me (John 15:26).

The Gift of the Holy Spirit

> But when He, the Spirit of truth, comes, He will guide you unto all the truth; for He will not speak on His own initiative, but whatever He hears, He will speak; and He will disclose to you what is to come (John 16:13).

These promises are different from the one Jesus made at the feast. It was to the apostles, not to all believers. It involved inspiration. They were to be guided into all truth and would remember all that Jesus had told them. The promise of the Holy Spirit was made to both the apostles and all believers. The purpose and scope of the promise, however, were not the same. "Receiving the Holy Spirit" is a phrase involving many different things.[2] It is a mistake to force the meaning of the phrase in one context to be identical with all other contexts.

Acts 2:38,39

Much of the discussion about the nature of the gift of the Holy Spirit centered around one passage of Scripture that promised the "gift of the Holy Spirit" upon baptism—Acts 2:38,39. Most everyone would agree that this "gift of the Holy Spirit" is received by a Christian when he is baptized. The disagreement comes because of a different understanding of what is involved in this "gift."

When Peter said, "You shall receive the gift of the Holy Spirit," what did he mean? Did he mean that the Holy Spirit *was* a gift from God that would dwell in the Christian? Did he mean that the Christian would *receive* a gift *from* the Holy Spirit?

Grammar does not show which it is. The phrase "of the Holy Spirit" *(tou hagiou pneumatos)* is in the genitive case. This does not help. If it is an "objective genitive," it would mean that the Holy Spirit *is* a gift from God to the Christian. If it is a "subjective genitive," it would mean that the Holy Spirit *gives* some sort of gift to the Christian.

The first thing A. T. Robertson says in *A Grammar of the Greek New Testament* (Nashville: Broadman Press, 1934, p. 499) is that the subjective genitive "can be distinguished

Alive in the Spirit!

from the objective use only by the context." The problem is that the immediate context of this passage does not indicate which it is. So, we must go to the broader context in Acts and the rest of the New Testament.

If the meaning of the text is that we receive a gift *from* the Holy Spirit Himself, there are two basic problems.

First, one has no idea of what the gift would be. Some have suggested that the gift was "salvation," "the Word of God" or "eternal life." That is subjective guessing. Neither this passage nor any other New Testament passage speaks of the Holy Spirit giving any such "gift" at baptism.

The conclusion we must draw from these plain passages is that the "gift of the Holy Spirit," promised to baptized believers on the day of Pentecost, is the Holy Spirit **Himself,** *who was given by God to everyone of His children, both then and now.*

Second, the only other time that the phrase "gift of the Holy Spirit" is used in the New Testament is with reference to the coming of the Holy Spirit on those at Cornelius' house in Caesarea. Luke recorded it thus: "And all the circumcised believers who had come with Peter were amazed, because the gift of the Holy Spirit had been poured out upon the Gentiles also."[3] This passage is clear on what the "gift of the Holy Spirit" is. It is the Holy Spirit Himself. The context of the passage proves it. The previous verse says, "the Holy Spirit fell upon all those who were listening to the message" (Acts 10:44). The "gift of the Holy Spirit" in this passage was a gift *from* God of the Holy Spirit.[4]

49

The Gift of the Holy Spirit

This is not to suggest that the way the Holy Spirit worked at Cornelius' house is the same way that He works upon those who receive the Holy Spirit at baptism. This is only to show that if the "gift of the Holy Spirit" referred to a gift from God of the Holy Spirit in one passage, it

The Word of God is clothed in human language. It is not a spiritual being but a neuter thing. It has no personality. It is used by the Holy Spirit to accomplish His work in the world. It is not, however, the Holy Spirit Himself.

would be likely that it also would refer to a gift from God of the Holy Spirit in another passage.

If the meaning of the text is that we receive the Holy Spirit Himself as a gift from God at baptism, numerous passages complement this understanding.

First, Peter referred to the Holy Spirit as a gift from God in his speech before the Council: "And we are witnesses of these things; and so is the Holy Spirit, whom God has given to those who obey Him" (Acts 5:32). Just as the coming of the Holy Spirit upon the apostles on Pentecost bore witness to the resurrection, so also in this context God's gift of the Holy Spirit "to those who obey Him" was a witness to His exaltation to the right hand of God.

Notice the text indicates that the Holy Spirit was a gift from God and that the Holy Spirit was given to those who obey.

Second, Paul affirmed that every child of God receives the Holy Spirit in Galatians. This is done in the context of how one becomes a child of God. One becomes a son of God "through faith in Christ Jesus." This is accomplished

Alive in the Spirit!

when one is "baptized into Christ" (Galatians 3:26,27). In the same context of discussing "sonship," Paul showed that sonship is connected to the Holy Spirit who dwells in the hearts of His children: "And because you are sons, God has sent forth the Spirit of His Son into our hearts, crying 'Abba! Father' " (Galatians 4:6)! The Holy Spirit that dwells in the heart of a Christian is evidence of sonship. God gives the Holy Spirit to a person when he, by faith and baptism, becomes one of His children.

Third, Paul affirms the indwelling of the Holy Spirit in the Christian's body. This is the basis of his argument he made to the Corinthians against the sin of fornication: "Or do you not know that your body is a temple of the Holy Spirit who is in you, whom you have from God, and that you are not your own" (1 Corinthians 6:19)? The Christian's body is holy because the Holy Spirit dwells in it. If you profane your body with fornication, then you are desecrating the temple of the Holy Spirit. The Holy Spirit that dwells *in* the Christian's body is *from God*.

Fourth, Paul made a direct statement about the indwelling of the Spirit in Romans. In the context of his discussion of life "according to the flesh" contrasted with life "according to the Spirit," he speaks of divinity dwelling in the children of God.

> However you are not in the flesh but in the Spirit, if indeed the *Spirit of God* dwells in you. But if anyone does not have the *Spirit of Christ*, he does not belong to Him. . . . But if the Spirit of Him who raised Jesus from the dead dwells in you, He who raised Christ Jesus from the dead will also give life to your mortal bodies through *His Spirit* who indwells you (Romans 8:9,11).

The text affirms that the Spirit of God and the Spirit of Christ dwell in those who are sons of God.[5] It should be no problem also to say that the Holy Spirit dwells in those who are sons of God.

Numerous other passages affirm the indwelling of the Holy Spirit in those who are Christians. The Holy Spirit,

The Gift of the Holy Spirit

Paul affirmed, has been "given to us" (Romans 5:5; Titus 3:5,6; 1 John 3:24); has been "given to you" (1 Thessalonians 4:8); and "dwells in us" (2 Timothy 1:14).

The conclusion we must draw from these plain passages is that the "gift of the Holy Spirit," promised to baptized believers on the day of Pentecost, is the Holy Spirit *Himself*, who was given by God to everyone of His children, both then and now.

The Holy Spirit and the Word of God

It is difficult to conceive of the indwelling of the Holy Spirit in a world understood by sense perception. Everything in the world seems to be timebound, takes up space and is governed by orderly physical laws. The very idea of a spiritual being that supercedes all of this is difficult to grasp.

It is also difficult not to react to the false claim that the Holy Spirit is involved in an emotional experience. Irrational behavior, illogical feelings and mystical experiences are thought by some to be the work of the Holy Spirit. When these are claimed, it is easy to react to the other extreme and want to make the work of the Holy Spirit something that can be confined to sense perception and human reasoning. It is, perhaps, this kind of background that has caused some to misunderstand the relationship of the Holy Spirit to the Word of God.

Does the Holy Spirit work only through the Word of God today? Is the Holy Spirit to be identified as the Bible? Does the Holy Spirit dwell in the Christian representatively through the Word of God? These real questions are asked about the Holy Spirit.

A clear distinction should be made between the Holy Spirit and the Word of God.

The Holy Spirit is God. He is a spiritual being of a different nature from anything or anybody in the physical world. He has inspired the men who spoke and wrote the Word of God (2 Peter 1:21), but He is not the Word of God. These inspired men who wrote the Scriptures have a relationship to the Holy Spirit much like a soldier has with his sword (Ephesians 6:17). One is the agent; the other is the instrument he uses.

The Word of God is clothed in human language. It is not a spiritual being but a neuter thing. It has no personality. It is used by the Holy Spirit to accomplish His work in the world. It is not, however, the Holy Spirit Himself. There are several dimensions in which the Holy Spirit and the Word of God are related.

First, we must understand that the source of the Word of God is the Holy Spirit. The Scriptures are "God breathed."[6]

The Word of God and the Holy Spirit are not the same. They are, however, related in their work in the world. The Holy Spirit inspired the Word of God, and the Word of God reveals the work of the Holy Spirit. The Holy Spirit is the agent, and the Word of God is the instrument of much of the Spirit's work in the world.

Men who wrote the Scriptures did not write merely what they thought or what they had learned from experience. They spoke from God. Peter affirmed this truth: ". . . for no prophecy was ever made by an act of human will, but men moved by the Holy Spirit spoke from God" (2 Peter 1:21). The Scriptures and the Holy Spirit cannot be separated any more than an agent can be separated from the instrument he uses.

When quoting from Scriptures, the writer of Hebrews said, "the Holy Spirit says" (Hebrews 3:7 quoting Psalm 95:7). He understood that David, the writer of the Psalm,

The Gift of the Holy Spirit

was inspired by the Holy Spirit. In one place he could say, "the Holy Spirit says," and in another place he could quote the same Scriptures and attribute it to David (see Hebrews 3:7; 4:7). The Holy Spirit and the Word of God are related but not identical.

Second, we must understand that the Holy Spirit does His work through the Word of God in many ways. Many of the things the Scriptures attribute to the Holy Spirit also are attributed to the Word of God. The following chart illustrates this.

Activity	Holy Spirit	Word of God
Birth	John 3:3,5	1 Peter 1:23
Saved	Titus 3:5	James 1:21
Sanctified	2 Thessalonians 2:13	John 17:17
Convicts	John 16:8-11	Acts 2:37
Guides	John 16:13	2 Timothy 3:15-17
Comforts	John 14:16-18	Romans 15:4

Many of the things done by the Holy Spirit are done through the Word of God. If you were to dig a hole with a shovel, it could be said that "a person dug the hole" or "the shovel dug the hole." Both would be correct. One statement would tell the "who." The other statement would tell the "instrument" that was used.

Third, we must understand that the Word of God reveals the work of the Holy Spirit. One would know nothing of the Holy Spirit were it not for the Word of God. Just as the Scriptures are "God breathed" by the Holy Spirit, the Holy Spirit is revealed by the Scriptures.

There is, in a certain sense, a revelation of divinity within man's own personality and within the created world. Paul says it this way:

> . . . because that which is known about God is evident within them; for God made it evident to them.

Alive in the Spirit!

For since the creation of the world His invisible attributes, His eternal power and divine nature, have been clearly seen, being understood through what has been made (Romans 1:19,20).

Some kind of knowledge of God can be known within man. The Greek philosophers reasoned that there must be a first cause. Some kind of knowledge of God can be known through nature. His power and orderliness are evident from natural observation of the universe. This was the message of David: "The heavens are telling of the glory of God; And their expanse is declaring the work of His hands" (Psalms 19:1). The majestic universe might declare the glory of God, but knowledge of the personality of God cannot be known except by revelation. The Holy Spirit would be unknown were it not for the Scriptures.

The Old Testament does not reveal much about the Holy Spirit. References to the Spirit are usually about God without indicating that the personality of the Holy Spirit is distinct from the Father and the Word. This is demonstrated in an event recorded by Luke in Acts.

At Ephesus Paul found 12 men who knew only the baptism of John (see Acts 19:1-7). He asked them, "Did you receive the Holy Spirit when you believed?" Their answer is revealing. They said, "No, we have not even heard whether there is a Holy Spirit." They knew about the preaching of John the Baptist but not about the Holy Spirit. Apollos, another follower of John the Baptist, was from this same area. He was mighty in the Old Testament Scriptures but did not know about Jesus or the Holy Spirit.

The Word of God and the Holy Spirit are not the same. They are, however, related in their work in the world. The Holy Spirit inspired the Word of God, and the Word of God reveals the work of the Holy Spirit. The Holy Spirit is the agent, and the Word of God is the instrument of much of the Spirit's work in the world. We will discuss this in more detail later.

The Gift of the Holy Spirit

Points of Confusion

The misunderstanding of the "gift of the Holy Spirit" is because of several points of confusion. Sometimes, men try to understand the gift of the Holy Spirit as a miracle, an experience or a neuter physical thing. The result is error.

The "gift of the Holy Spirit" promised to all baptized believers is not a miracle in the New Testament sense.[7] It is a promise of God fulfilled at baptism like the forgiveness of sins.

The gift of the Holy Spirit is no more a miracle than is the forgiveness of sins. Both are from God. Both are marvelous. Both are promised. Both are known because of faith in the promises of God. You know you have the forgiveness of sins when you are baptized in the name of Jesus Christ because the Bible promised it. In the same way, you know you have the gift of the Holy Spirit. You do not need a miracle to know this; God's promise is sufficient. Indeed, if one does not believe the Scriptures, he would not believe a miracle. That was Abraham's response to the rich man in Hades: "If they do not listen to Moses and the Prophets, neither will they be persuaded if someone rises from the dead" (Luke 16:31).

God promises the "gift of the Holy Spirit" to baptized believers in the Scriptures—God's laws of revelation. You can trust the promises in the laws of revelation just as much as you can trust the laws of creation in nature. God does His work in an orderly and consistent way. He is trustworthy. You can believe His promises. Because the "gift of the Holy Spirit" is a promise of God given in a consistent way as revealed in Scriptures, it is not a miracle.

The "gift of the Holy Spirit" promised to all baptized believers is not an emotional experience. To identify it as such is a form of idolatry. Just as ancient pagans sought to make gods in human physical forms, modern idolaters seek to make the Holy Spirit into human emotional experiences. Both are wrong. God is a spiritual being, not a human form or a human emotion.

Alive in the Spirit!

Identifying the Holy Spirit with human emotional experience presents some very difficult logical problems.

First, how does one know the experience is from God? It could be from another source. John warns that one is not to believe every spirit because many false prophets have gone out into the world (1 John 4:1). The Bible that teaches about the Holy Spirit affirms that there are also evil or unholy spirits.

The experience might be from one's own psyche. After all, a man's mind and emotions work in odd ways. A man can dream dreams; he can feel the heights of exultation; he can feel the depths of depression; he can have hunches; he can feel fears; and his spirit can be excited to produce irrational behavior. All of this is within the realm of human experience. There is nothing wrong with such experiences because they are a part of the makeup of a man. They, of themselves, are neither bad nor good.

Leaders of the Greek mystery religions used such experiences to convince their followers that the gods possessed them. In their literature we find tongue speaking, divine healing, spirit possession, exorcism and other emotional experiences as evidence of the gods' dwelling in them. They were concerned with "obtaining an experience." They prompted these experiences by gory rituals, sensual music, suggestive drama, hypnotic ceremonies and sometimes even drugs. We must not confuse experiential, emotional feelings with divine reality.

Human emotional experiences are both changing and contradictory. A person's feelings change with time. One person's experiences are contradictory to another person's experiences. This is the reason that those who look to human emotional experiences for religious certainty cannot agree with one another. This is the reason that the same emotional experience is interpreted differently by different people at different times. Human emotional experiences cannot be identified with the "gift of the Holy Spirit."

The gift of the Holy Spirit promised to all baptized believers is not a physical entity. The Holy Spirit is not bound in time or space because He is God.

The Gift of the Holy Spirit

The idea that the Holy Spirit is a physical entity probably evolved from the idea that the "gift of the Holy Spirit" is, in reality, a gift *from* the Holy Spirit and that this gift possesses physical qualities. Closely connected with this idea is that the Holy Spirit is received by "measure" or degrees. (This will be discussed in Chapter 6.) It is foolish to suggest that the promise of the Holy Spirit dwelling in every Christian is some kind of physical element, then, on the basis of this false assumption, say that this would divide divinity. The Holy Spirit Himself can dwell in as many places at one time as He wants. He is God. He is not limited in time and space or even by man's own limited understanding of His nature.

It is a quibble to charge that if the Holy Spirit dwells in a Christian, then it would be God incarnate. It is uncritical to suggest that if the Holy Spirit dwells in a Christian, then people should worship him as God in the flesh. Such indwelling, it is contended, not only makes God (the Word) become flesh in Jesus Christ, but also God (the Spirit) dwell in the flesh-and-blood Christian. There is a difference in Jesus' "sharing in flesh and blood" and a spirit's dwelling in one's body. Good *and* bad spirits can dwell in a person. This does not make him weigh more or look different. A spirit is not of the same nature as flesh and blood (see Luke 24:39). The incarnation of Jesus was different. He became "like His brethren in all things" (Hebrews 2:14-18).

When we understand that the Holy Spirit is not some kind of physical entity, we will be better able to understand the promise of the Scriptures that the Holy Spirit does dwell in a Christian. God fulfills the promise of giving the gift of the Holy Spirit as well as the forgiveness of sins to every believer who repents and is baptized in the name of Jesus Christ.

We can know this by faith. We do not have to have an emotional experience or receive some kind of proof from a miracle. We do not have to observe some physical evidence that can be measured. We know it because the Bible says it. We know the Holy Spirit dwells in us in the

Alive in the Spirit!

same way that we know God has forgiven our sins. We believe the promises.

Study Questions

1. Discuss the difference between Jesus' promise of the Holy Spirit to the apostles and the promise given to all Christians in Acts 2:38.
2. How can we know that the promise of the Holy Spirit received by all Christians is the Holy Spirit Himself that is given from God as a gift?
3. Compare the "gift of the Holy Spirit" found in Acts 2:38 and Acts 10:45 with "gifts of the Holy Spirit" found in Hebrews 2:4.
4. Discuss at least six ways the Holy Spirit works through the Word of God in doing His work in the world.
5. How can we know we have received the gift of the Holy Spirit?
6. Show how emotional experience is not evidence of receiving the Holy Spirit.
7. Show how receiving the gift of the Holy Spirit is not a miracle.
8. Memory work: Acts 2:38.

End Notes

[1] Jesus also told the Samaritan woman that He had power to give "living water." See John 4:10.

[2] It can refer to enhancing natural skills (Exodus 31:3; Judges 14:6). It can refer to inspiration (2 Peter 1:20,21). It can refer to the promise of the Holy Spirit at baptism (Acts 2:38). It can refer to the reception of the Holy Spirit through the laying on of the apostles' hands (Acts 8:18). It can refer to "grace gifts" possessed by Christians at Rome and Corinth (1 Corinthians 12:1-11; Romans 12:6-8).

[3] Acts 10:45. The plural, "gifts" of the Holy Spirit is found in most translations in Hebrews 2:4, but an entirely different Greek term is used. The term *merismos*, meaning "distributions," is used in Hebrews 2:4 while the term *dorea*, meaning "gift," is used in Acts 2:38 and Acts 10:45.

[4] Acts 11:17 shows that the source of the gift was God. Peter said to the Jewish brethren in Jerusalem, "If God therefore gave to them the same gift as He gave to us also after believing in the Lord Jesus Christ, who was I that I could stand in God's way?"

[5] The term "Holy Spirit" is not in this chapter. The emphasis is on the work of the divine Spirit. Sometimes He is referred to as the "Spirit of God." Sometimes He is referred to as the "Spirit of Christ." Most often He is just referred to as "the Spirit."

[6] 2 Timothy 3:16. The word translated "inspired by God" in this passage is *theopneustos*, which literally means "God breathed."

The Gift of the Holy Spirit

⁷A miracle in the New Testament has God as its source and confirmation of a man and/or his message as its purpose. It is supernatural in nature, that is, not according to God's laws of creation and revelation. For a full discussion of miracles see Jimmy Jividen, *Miracles, From God or Man?* (Abilene: ACU Press, 1987), pp. 1-10.

SIX

Measures of the Holy Spirit

Different "measures of the Holy Spirit" is an analogy that is sometimes used to describe the way the Holy Spirit has worked in the world. Even a superficial reading of New Testament passages on the Holy Spirit shows that He did not work in the same way in every individual in all situations. The immediate question is "Why?"

We could hardly say that He who moved upon the face of the waters in creation to bring order out of chaos would be inconsistent in His work in the lives of people. We certainly would not contradict Scripture to suggest that the Holy Spirit is a respecter of persons (Acts 10:34). How can we then explain that some were "baptized with the Holy Spirit," others received the Holy Spirit through the "laying on of the apostles' hands" and others received the "gift of the Holy Spirit" at baptism. We seek to know "How?" and "Why?"

Different Works of the Holy Spirit

A careful study of the Scriptures answers most of these questions. There was order, purpose and consistency in the way the Holy Spirit worked in the lives of men. The following chart outlines most of the activity of the Holy Spirit recorded in the New Testament.

Measures of the Holy Spirit

Who	How	Why
Apostles and Cornelius	Baptism of Holy Spirit	Confirmation from God
Selected Christians	Laying on of the apostles' hands	Receive spiritual gifts
All Christians	By baptism	Receive the gift of the Holy Spirit

Nowhere does the Scripture outline the work of the Holy Spirit in such categories. These categories do, however, fit what the Scriptures say about the Holy Spirit.

As already shown in Chapter 4 baptism with the Holy Spirit was received by the apostles on the day of Pentecost in Jerusalem and by Cornelius while Peter was preaching to him at Caesarea. Its purpose at Jerusalem was to show God's sanction of the apostles and their message. Its purpose at Caesarea was to show God's sanction of Peter's preaching to the Gentiles and baptizing Cornelius and his household (see Acts 2:33; 10:46,47; 11:17,18). This fits the first category of the chart.

Certain Christians, during the days of the apostles, received spiritual gifts through the laying on of the apostles' hands.[1] This is evident because Luke records that two of the seven men who received the laying on of the apostles' hands in Acts 6 were able to work miracles (Acts 6:8; 8:6). The statements of Luke are plain:

> Now when the apostles in Jerusalem heard that Samaria had received the word of God, they sent them Peter and John, who came down and prayed for them, that they might receive the Holy Spirit. For He had not yet fallen upon any of them; they had simply been baptized in the name of the Lord Jesus (Acts 8:14-16).
>
> Now when Simon saw that the Spirit was bestowed through the laying on of the apostles' hands, he

Alive in the Spirit!

offered them money, saying "give this authority to me as well" (Acts 8:18,19).

The Samaritans who had been baptized had already received the "gift of the Holy Spirit" according to the promise Peter made on Pentecost (Acts 2:38). There was a different way by which the Holy Spirit was received through the laying on of the apostles' hands. A different purpose was involved.

The laying on of an apostle's hands gave power to 12 men at Ephesus by which they could "speak in tongues" and "prophecy" (Acts 19:6). The laying on of Paul's hands was the means by which Timothy obtained a "gift of God" (2 Timothy 1:6).

It is significant that the church at Corinth was "not lacking in any spiritual gift" after an apostle had been present with them for more than a year (1 Corinthians 1:7). The church at Rome, which had no recorded visit from an apostle up to the time Paul wrote, still needed to have spiritual gifts imparted to them by Paul (Romans 1:11).

These Scriptures confirm the second category of the chart, showing that certain individuals received special powers of the Holy Spirit through the laying on of the apostles' hands.

Every penitent believer in Jesus Christ who is baptized receives the "gift of the Holy Spirit." The nature of this gift has been discussed already in Chapter 5. This work of the Holy Spirit fits into a different category from the other two. It is given to all who will obey the Lord in baptism—not to just apostles or those who receive the laying on of their hands. It is non-miraculous—those who possess it do not prophesy, speak in tongues or work miracles. It is not limited to the first century but is extended to all whom the Lord calls.

This possession of the Holy Spirit is the basis of sonship in God's family (see Galatians 4:6). He is the tie that binds members of the body together in unity (1 Corinthians 12:13). He is the basis of holiness of one's physical body

Measures of the Holy Spirit

(1 Corinthians 6:19). He is the basis for the sanctity of the church (1 Corinthians 3:16). Scriptures confirm this category of the working of the Holy Spirit.

The chart shows categories of the working of the Holy Spirit of God. Understanding these categories keeps us from attributing the special work of the Holy Spirit upon certain persons in the first century to individuals in the 20th century.

John 3:34

An analogy is used sometimes to explain the different categories of the work of the Holy Spirit. It is the idea that the Holy Spirit is received by measure or degrees. The passage used as a basis for this analogy is a statement of Jesus: "For He whom God has sent speaks the words of God; for He gives the Spirit without measure. The Father loves the Son, and has given all things into His hand" (John 3:34,35). The passage is thought to teach that Jesus received the Holy Spirit without measure.[2] It is suggested then that the apostles received another measure when they were baptized in the Holy Spirit. Those on whom the apostles laid hands received another measure. Those who are baptized believers receive another measure.[3] This analogy adds one new category to the above chart. It is the category of Jesus who received the Spirit without measure.

Such an analogy divides the operation of the Holy Spirit into logical categories. The Holy Spirit has operated in different ways at different times and upon different groups of individuals.

Because the idea of "measure" often involves a measurement of physical things, some have the idea that the Holy Spirit is a physical thing that can be measured. One measure of the Holy Spirit is given to one, and a different measure of the Holy Spirit is given to another. Does this passage teach a physical view of the Holy Spirit? Certainly not. The Holy Spirit is not a thing to be measured. He is God and cannot be divided into portions.

Alive in the Spirit!

A close look at the text, "He gives the Spirit without measure" causes us to consider several ideas.

First, who is the giver of the Holy Spirit? It would appear that God is the giver.[4] The first part of the verse refers to God's sending Jesus. The following verse refers to God's giving all things into Jesus' hands. It would seem then that the giver of the Holy Spirit without measure would be God.

It is true that the pronoun "He" is used by John the Baptist to refer to Jesus in the broad context.[5]

> He must increase, but I must decrease . . .
> He who comes from above is above all . . .
> What He has seen and heard, of that He bears witness . . .
> He whom God has sent speaks the words of God . . .
> (John 3:30-34).

The most immediate context, however, refers to "God the sender" of Jesus and "God the giver" of all things to Jesus. We must leave the immediate context to claim anyone but God as the giver of the Spirit without measure.

It is true that the Scriptures teach that Jesus is the one who will baptize with the Holy Spirit (Matthew 3:11). It is also true that Jesus was later to make a promise that He would send the Holy Spirit: "When the Helper comes, whom I will send to you from the Father, that is the Spirit of truth . . . He will bear witness of Me" (John 15:26).

Jesus is the giver of the Spirit in this passage. Jesus is also the one who will baptize with the Holy Spirit.

Is Jesus, therefore, the giver of the Holy Spirit without measure? Not necessarily. A multitude of passages also speak of the Father's being the giver of the Holy Spirit (see John 14:16,17,26; 15:26; Acts 2:33). Who gives the Spirit without measure must be identified in the passage itself. Not denying that Jesus is the giver of the Holy Spirit in other contexts, the immediate context here would suggest that God was the giver of the Spirit without measure.

Measures of the Holy Spirit

Second, the verb translated "gives" is in the present tense.[6] The use of this tense would indicate that the Holy Spirit who was given "without measure" is still in the process of being given. It does not refer to one event in the past, like the baptism of Jesus, at which the Spirit of God descended on Jesus (Matthew 3:16). It is the progressive present—that is past action still in progress.[7]

Third, the use of the phrase "without measure" does not demand that the Holy Spirit be understood as a physical quantity.

The Holy Spirit is not something to be measured out as one would measure jars of water or bushels of wheat.

The spiritual gifts were from the Holy Spirit. They were not all the same. Different Christians possessed different gifts. The diversity of gifts was not a sign of holiness of the receiver but of the sovereign will of the Spirit who gave the gifts. The purpose was for the common good of all in the body.

He is God and is not limited by time or space as a physical creation. He is Spirit and does not have flesh and bones or other aspects of this physical world. He is personality and cannot be divided.

Deissner, in his article "Metron" in *The Theological Dictionary of the New Testament* (Grand Rapids: Wm. B. Eerdmans, 1973), indicates the meaning of "without measure" in this passage to be "without restriction." He quotes from Rabbi Acha: "The Holy Ghost himself, who rests on the prophets, rests (on them) only by weight (measure); one of them prophesied one book, another (like Jeremiah)

Alive in the Spirit!

two." The Holy Spirit worked in the life and ministry of Jesus without the restrictive limits with which He had worked in priests and prophets. He worked in Jesus without the limitations that were and are involved in His work in other people.

This teaching must not be perverted to make the Holy Spirit a physical thing. One physical measure of the Holy Spirit is not poured into one person and another physical measure poured into another person. We do not measure the Holy Spirit of God by human standards. We do not use an analogy in a literal sense.

Distributions of the Spirit

The Holy Spirit worked in a variety of ways in the New Testament church. This is seen particularly in the spiritual gifts.[8] Different gifts were given to different Christians for the good of the whole. There was unity of the gifts in their source—the Holy Spirit (1 Corinthians 12:4,7-9,11). There was unity of the gifts in their purpose—the common good (1 Corinthians 12:7). There was diversity of gifts—given by the will of the Holy Spirit (1 Corinthians 12:11). Different words in the following passage are emphasized to show the different distribution of gifts from the Holy Spirit.

> Now there are *varieties* of gifts, but the same Spirit. There are *varieties* of ministries, and the same Lord. And there are *varieties* of effects, but the same God who works all things in all persons. But *to each one is given* the manifestation of the Spirit for the common good. For *to one is given* the word of wisdom through the Spirit, and *to another* the word of knowledge according to the same Spirit; *to another* faith by the same Spirit, and *to another* the gift of healing by the one Spirit, and *to another* the effecting of miracles, and *to another* prophecy, and *to another* the distinguishing of spirits, *to another* various kinds of tongues, and *to another* the interpretation of tongues. But one and the same Spirit works all these things, *distributing to each* one individually just as He wills (1 Corinthians 12:4-11).

Measures of the Holy Spirit

The spiritual gifts were from the Holy Spirit. They were not all the same. Different Christians possessed different gifts. The diversity of the gifts was not a sign of holiness of the receiver but of the sovereign will of the Spirit who gave the gifts. The purpose was for the common good of all in the body.

The Holy Spirit is not something to be measured out as one would measure jars of water or bushels of wheat. He is God and is not limited by time or space as a physical creation. He is Spirit and does not have flesh and bones or other aspects of this physical world. He is personality and cannot be divided.

There were no physical measures of the Holy Spirit involved in this distribution. Possessing one gift did not put one over the others or mean that the Holy Spirit worked more powerfully in one than the other. The Holy Spirit worked totally in each individual who possessed a gift. The gift one had was different from the gift others had. It was no less a work of the Holy Spirit because it was different.

Distribution of gifts from the Holy Spirit is also indicated in another passage. In the context of how the salvation that first was spoken through the Lord received confirmation through miracles, the book of Hebrews speaks of distributions of the Holy Spirit: "God also bearing witness with them, both by signs and wonders and by various

Alive in the Spirit!

miracles and by gifts of the Holy Spirit according to His own will" (Hebrews 2:4).

The word translated "gifts" is *merismos*. A literal meaning of this word would be "distributions." The text says that the Holy Spirit, according to His own will, made distribution of gifts. These gifts involved signs and wonders to confirm the message spoken by the Lord.

These two passages indicate that the Holy Spirit was the giver of miraculous gifts to certain individuals in the New Testament for the confirmation of revelation. These different gifts were distributed to different individuals according to the will of the Holy Spirit.

There is a difference between the concept of the Holy Spirit's being the distributor of gifts to individuals and individuals receiving measures of the Holy Spirit.

In the New Testament the "distribution of the Holy Spirit" means gifts given by the Holy Spirit. There were different gifts to different individuals, but the source was the Holy Spirit. All of this is involved in a statement of Paul: "But one and the same Spirit works all these things, distributing to each one individually just as He wills" (1 Corinthians 12:11).

The word "measure" is connected to the Holy Spirit only one time in the New Testament. Then it is used with the negative, "without measure." It refers to the unrestricted power of the Holy Spirit's working in Jesus. Never is "measure" used in a positive way to refer to a portion or measure of the Holy Spirit working in an individual. There is no New Testament reference to the "baptismal measure" or the "miraculous measure."

The idea of "measure" usually conveys a dividing of the whole. When such a term is used with reference to the positive work of the Holy Spirit two problems arise. First, there is no textual support of the idea. Second, such a use of the term would seem to divide the Holy Spirit into portions.

The "measure" analogy in describing the different activities of the Holy Spirit in different people at different times and for different purposes certainly can be used as an

Measures of the Holy Spirit

illustration. It must be remembered that it is just an illustration to show such differences and must not be taken literally. An analogy taken to the extreme will ultimately break down.

The idea of physical "measures" of the Holy Spirit is without a Scriptural basis. The idea of "measures of the Holy Spirit" has traditionally been used as an analogy to illustrate how He works in different ways in different people at different times. This has been helpful in bringing better understanding of the biblical doctrine. If this analogy is taken literally or is taken to its ultimate extreme, it can produce error.

Study Questions

1. Discuss the different ways the Holy Spirit has worked since the ascension of Jesus. Show what persons and purposes were involved in each way.
2. What is the meaning of Jesus' receiving the Holy Spirit "without measure?"
3. What kind of gifts are given by the Holy Spirit? What are their purposes? What determines their reception?
4. What allowed the apostles power to lay hands on individuals in order for them to receive the Holy Spirit?
5. Should one refer to the different works of the Holy Spirit as "measures of the Spirit?"
6. Show the differences in the grace gifts at Rome and Corinth as given in Romans 12:6-8 and 1 Corinthians 12:4-31. What explanation might be made for their differences?
7. Does the work of the Holy Spirit today require anything miraculous? Does it require any kind of emotional feeling?
8. Memory work: John 3:34.

End Notes

[1] The power that the apostles had to bestow such gifts did not come from the baptism of the Holy Spirit. It came from their apostolic office (see 2 Corinthians 12:12). Cornelius could not bestow gifts, only those who were apostles.

[2] This understanding is based on the King James Version (KJV), which says, "for God giveth not the Spirit by measure *unto Him.*" The italics are not in the Greek text, and one cannot prove from the language whether the giver of the Spirit is the Father or Jesus.

Alive in the Spirit!

[3] J. W. Roberts, "The Holy Spirit," *Restoration Quarterly* XVII, 1, 1974, pp. 36-38.

[4] It must be conceded that the reading of "God" instead of "He" in verse 34 that is found in the KJV is without solid textual basis. Such is not found in the earliest or best manuscripts. The phrase "unto Him" in the KJV is also without textual support.

[5] The view has been taken by some that the one who was to give the Spirit without measure was Jesus. See Richard Rogers, *A Study of the Holy Spirit of God* (Lubbock: Richard Rogers, 1968), p. 20. See Bruce Terry, "Baptized in One Spirit," *Restoration Quarterly* XXI, 4, 1978, pp. 193-200.

[6] The word is *didosin*. The present tense is the tense of progressive action and present time.

[7] A. T. Robertson, *A Grammar of the Greek New Testament* (Nashville: Broadman Press, 1923), pp. 879, 880.

[8] The word translated "spiritual gifts" in 1 Corinthians 12:4 is *charismaton*, which literally means "grace gifts." The meaning of the word does not imply the miraculous but that which is freely given. The word is used of the non-miraculous gifts enumerated in Romans 12:6-8. In the Romans passage, the Holy Spirit is not mentioned, but emphasis is placed on the grace by which the gifts are given. The same is true of Ephesians 4:4-11. The grace by which one receives the different gifts is emphasized. In the Ephesians passage, Jesus, not the Holy Spirit, is the giver.

SEVEN

Indwelling of the Holy Spirit

The study of pagan religions, especially the Greek and Roman mystery religions, reveals that men seek to be possessed by divinity. Those in the ancient Dionysus cult would seek to gain a "god-in-ness" through drinking wine. When the spirit of the wine caused them to feel "beside themselves," they would believe they were possessed by the gods.

The "taurobolium" was a rite used in the Attis cult. It consisted of a platform-like altar on which a bull was sacrificed. The person being initiated into the cult would stand under the platform and be covered in the blood that gushed from the butchered animal. Blood would run into his eyes, ears and mouth. This ceremony was supposed to bring a "god-in-ness." These pagans wanted to be possessed by the gods. The state of ecstasy or drunkenness these pagan worshipers achieved was a strong delusion. They believed a lie. Their irrational rituals show, however, the universal quest for divinity.

Other cults would use drama, gory rituals and other emotionally stimulating methods to induce a religious experience. They then would interpret this experience to be the "indwelling of god."

The English word "enthusiasm" no doubt had its origin in such an experience. It is a combination of two Greek words, *"en,"* and *"theos,"* which literally means "in god" or "god in." The exuberance produced by these pagan religious experiences was understood as being the indwelling of god.

Alive in the Spirit!

What ancient pagans sought from false gods by counterfeit means is to be found in a reality by children of God. God dwells in His church and His people.

Old Testament Predictions

The Old Testament does not give clear indications of the Holy Spirit's being a personality distinct from God. The Old Testament does refer to God and the Spirit in different ways, but it was not until God's revelation in the New Testament that one finds a clear understanding of the Holy Spirit.

The Old Testament speaks of the Spirit of God being active in creation (Genesis 1:2; Psalms 104:28-30). Prophets recognized that their message was not their own but that of the Spirit of God (2 Samuel 23:2; Ezekiel 2:2; 8:3; 11:1; Isaiah 61:1; Jeremiah 1:4. See also 2 Peter 1:21).

The Spirit of God gave extraordinary power to different individuals to accomplish the bidding of the Lord. Those who built the tabernacle received the Spirit of God to enhance their workmanship (Exodus 31:3). The Spirit of God came upon the judges to give them strength and leadership (Judges 6:34; 11:29; 14:6).

The Old Testament prophesied that the Spirit of God one day would work in the world more fully. Three passages illustrate this. The first refers to the Spirit's coming upon the promised Messiah. The second refers to the Spirit's coming upon the seed of Jacob. The third refers to the Spirit's coming upon all flesh.

The Spirit would rest upon the Messiah. Isaiah predicted it:

> The Spirit of the Lord God is upon me, Because the Lord has anointed me to bring good news to the afflicted; He has sent me to bind up the brokenhearted, to proclaim liberty to captives, and freedom to prisoners; to proclaim the favorable year of our God (Isaiah 61:1,2).

Indwelling of the Holy Spirit

This passage reflected the ministry of Jesus. Jesus responded to the disciples of John when they inquired if He were the "Coming One" by quoting this passage (Matthew 11:4,5).

Early in His ministry Jesus returned to His hometown of Nazareth. As His custom was, He went into the synagogue on the Sabbath day. He was asked to read the Scriptures. The place He chose to read was this passage. After reading it He sat down and said, "Today this Scripture has been fulfilled in your hearing" (Luke 4:21). Jesus recognized that He was the Messiah of whom Isaiah spoke and the one upon whom the Holy Spirit would rest.

The Spirit would rest upon the seed of Jacob. Isaiah predicted that a Redeemer would come to Zion. Those who turned from the transgression of Jacob would be part of a covenant with God that involved His Spirit resting upon them.

> And a Redeemer will come to Zion, and to those who turn from transgression in Jacob, declares the Lord. And as for Me, This is My covenant with them, says the Lord: My Spirit which is upon you, and My words which I have put in your mouth, shall not depart . . . from now and forever (Isaiah 59:20,21).

Paul quoted this passage from Isaiah and showed that it applies to Israel (Romans 11:26,27). He showed that what God promised Isaiah was fulfilled in his time. God did establish a covenant with those who turned from the transgression of Jacob, and His Spirit did rest upon them.

The Spirit would rest upon all mankind. This was the prophecy of Joel: "And it shall be in the last days, God says, that I will pour forth of My Spirit upon all mankind" (Joel 2:28-32).

Peter on the day of Pentecost said, "This is what was spoken of through the prophet Joel" (Acts 2:16-22). What the multitude saw and heard happening to the apostles was a fulfillment of this prophecy. The Spirit would be given to all mankind. This fulfillment also was to be seen in the promise Peter made at the close of his sermon:

Alive in the Spirit!

". . . and you shall receive the gift of the Holy Spirit. For the promise is for you and your children, and for all who are far off, as many as the Lord our God shall call to Himself" (Acts 2:38,39).

The passage was fulfilled also when those at the household of Cornelius received the Holy Spirit (Acts 11:15). Joel's prediction of the Spirit's being poured out upon all mankind had come to pass.

God Dwells in His Children

God in a real sense dwells in those who are His children. This is the promise of the Scripture. The fact that we cannot see, hear, feel or emotionally experience this indwelling of the Holy Spirit in a physical way does not negate the promise of God. We know that God dwells in us because the Bible tells us so.

A spirit does not have physical characteristics to be discerned by the five senses. A man cannot prove or disprove the presence of a spirit by scientific examination. A spirit does not take up space, nor is he limited in time.

The doctrine that the Holy Spirit works through the Word of God is a biblical doctrine. The doctrine that the Holy Spirit works through the Word of God only is false.

Man exists in a different dimension from spiritual beings. This does not make spirits less real but only limits man's ability to understand their nature.

The only thing we can know about the Holy Spirit or any spiritual being is through the revelation of God. Because Jesus said, ". . . a spirit has not flesh and bones" (Luke 24:39), I believe it. Because Jesus said, "God is

Indwelling of the Holy Spirit

spirit" (John 4:24), I accept it. Because the Scriptures say angels are "ministering spirits" (Hebrews 1:14), I know it is true. Because Peter promised those who repented and were baptized, "You shall receive the gift of the Holy Spirit" (Acts 2:38), I acknowledge that it's true.

God dwells in him who loves his brother (1 John 4:12). Christ dwells in our hearts through faith (Ephesians 3:17). The Holy Spirit dwells in those who are living "in the Spirit" (Romans 8:9). Divinity *can* dwell in humanity.

John gave three criteria by which we can know if God abides in us. The first is to "love one another." The second is the "indwelling of His Spirit." The third is the confession that "Jesus is the Son of God."

> No one has beheld God at any time; if we love one another, God abides in us, and His love is perfected in us. By this we know that we abide in Him and He in us, because He has given us of His Spirit . . . Whoever confesses that Jesus is the Son of God, God abides in him, and he in God (1 John 4:12-15).[1]

The indwelling of God, Christ and the Holy Spirit is not something that can be known through emotional experiences; it can only be determined by the criteria set forth by John.

The Holy Spirit Dwells in the Christian

There should be no difficulty in accepting the personal or real indwelling of the Holy Spirit. The Scriptures are plain. It already has been shown in Chapter 5 that Peter promised the Holy Spirit to those who became Christians on the day of Pentecost. God was the giver, and the Holy Spirit was the gift (Acts 5:32; Galatians 4:6).

In an even more graphic way, Peter declared that the Holy Spirit dwells in the Christian's body. This is the argument he made to the Corinthians against immorality. The Christian's body is holy because it is the temple of the Holy Spirit. To use the body for immorality is to desecrate the temple of the Holy Spirit.

> Or do you not know that your body is a temple of the Holy Spirit who is in you, whom you have from God, and you are not your own? For you have been bought with a price: therefore glorify God in your body (1 Corinthians 6:19,20).

The language of the text shows that the Holy Spirit is in the body, and He is a gift from God.

The Holy Spirit is a partial payment on the eternal inheritance promised to the Christian. Possession of the Holy Spirit assures us that we have a legal claim to all God has promised. Something bigger and better awaits us in the future. The pledge of the Holy Spirit is a foretaste of it all.

The understanding that the Holy Spirit dwells in a Christian does not create any theological problems in regard to the free will of man or the non-miraculous working of God in the world today.[2]

The indwelling of the Holy Spirit is described four ways in the Scriptures.

First, He is a gift from God. That is the promise Peter made to those who were pricked in their hearts on the day of Pentecost: "Repent and let each of you be baptized in the name of Jesus Christ for the forgiveness of your sins; and *you shall receive the gift of the Holy Spirit*" (Acts 2:38). Luke recorded another statement of Peter in the Acts narrative in which the giver of the Holy Spirit is

Indwelling of the Holy Spirit

identified. In his defense before the Council, Peter boldly stated this: "And we are witnesses of these things; and so is the Holy Spirit, whom *God has given* to those who obey Him" (Acts 5:32). The Holy Spirit is God's gift to those who obey Him. He is a Helper whom God has given to those who are His children. The Christian has an advantage because he has the help of divinity.

Second, the Holy Spirit is the seal of the New Covenant, much as circumcision was the seal of the Old Covenant.

Fleshly birth made one a Jew. The Jews were the people of God in the Old Testament. Circumcision was the sign or seal of that Old Covenant that God made with them. God commanded it of Abraham.

> This is My covenant, which you shall keep, between Me and you and your descendants after you: every male among you shall be circumcised. And you shall be circumcised in the flesh of your foreskin; and it shall be a sign of the covenant between Me and you (Genesis 17:10,11).

Circumcision was the seal of the Old Covenant. It, like any seal, authenticated the covenant as genuine. Those who received this seal were in a covenant relationship with God. Circumcision was a physical sign to show that one belonged to God and that God would fulfill the conditions of the covenant.

Paul used the same covenant terms with reference to the Holy Spirit's being the sign or seal of the New Covenant:

> In Him, you also, after listening to the message of truth, the gospel of your salvation—having also believed, you were sealed in Him with the Holy Spirit of promise (Ephesians 1:13).

> And do not grieve the Holy Spirit of God, by whom you were sealed for the day of redemption (Ephesians 4:30).

Alive in the Spirit!

The Holy Spirit is the seal of the New Covenant, just as circumcision was the seal of the Old Covenant. Like circumcision, the Holy Spirit is the sign that we are in a covenant relationship with God. The Holy Spirit, on man's side, is a sign that we belong to God, and on God's side that He will fulfill all of the conditions promised in the New Covenant.[3]

Third, the Holy Spirit is a pledge. He is so described in three passages.

> . . . sealed in Him with the Holy Spirit of promise, who is given as a pledge of our inheritance, with a view to the redemption of God's own possession, to the praise of His glory (Ephesians 1:13,14).
>
> Now He who established us with you in Christ and anointed us is God, who also sealed us and gave us the Spirit in our hearts as a pledge (2 Corinthians 1:21,22).
>
> Now He who prepared us for this very purpose is God, who gave us the Spirit as a pledge . . . (2 Corinthians 5:5).

The Holy Spirit is a pledge God has given to the Christian that assures his full redemption and salvation. The Holy Spirit is, in contemporary economic language, a "down payment" that God has given now but which anticipates full payment in glory. The definition of the Greek word *arrabon* is as follows:

> The word is a commercial term. . . . It signifies a "pledge" which is later returned (only Genesis 38:17-20); a "deposit" which pays part of the total debt and gives a legal claim; . . . "earnest-money" ratifying a compact . . . It always implies an act which engages to something bigger.[4]

The Holy Spirit is a partial payment on the eternal inheritance promised to the Christian. Possession of the Holy Spirit assures us that we have a legal claim to all God has promised. Something bigger and better awaits

Indwelling of the Holy Spirit

us in the future. The pledge of the Holy Spirit is a foretaste of it all.

The context of 2 Corinthians 5:1-5 confirms this thought. In this passage Paul wrote of "groaning" in the earthly tabernacle of the body and wishing for a "building from God, a house not made with hands, eternal in the heavens." While Christians wait for this heavenly house, they have a pledge from God of the Holy Spirit.

The context of Ephesians 1:14 conveys the same thought. The Holy Spirit is spoken of as a pledge from God that a Christian has until he receives his full inheritance and full redemption.

A similar thought is conveyed under the phrase, "first fruits of the Spirit." It is used only one time in the New Testament:

> For we know that the whole creation groans and suffers the pains of childbirth together until now. And not only this, but also we ourselves, having the first fruits of the Spirit, even we ourselves groan within ourselves, waiting eagerly for our adoption as sons, the redemption of our body (Romans 8:22,23).

The Holy Spirit is God's pledge to us as Christians that something bigger and better awaits us in heaven.

Fourth, the Holy Spirit is the mark to identify us as being in the family of God. He is the basis of the relationship that God has with His children. He is also the bond of brotherhood between all the children in the family.

We are born into God's family at baptism. By giving the Holy Spirit to the one who is "born again," God affirms, "This is My Child!" We are identified with the family. Paul affirmed this:

> For you are all sons of God through faith in Christ Jesus. For all of you who were baptized into Christ have clothed yourselves with Christ . . . And because you are sons, God has sent forth the Spirit of His Son into our hearts, crying, *"Abba!* Father" (Galatians 3:26,27; 4:6).

Alive in the Spirit!

Faith and baptism make us sons of God. At this time the Spirit is given by God to those who are sons. This is the basis by which they can call God "Father." The basis of this relationship does not consist of genes or environment. The basis is the Holy Spirit.

The indwelling of the Holy Spirit as a basis for family identity is also shown in Romans:

> For all who are being led by the Spirit of God, these are sons of God. For you have not received a spirit of slavery leading to fear again, but you have received a spirit of adoption as sons by which we cry out, "*Abba!* Father!" The Spirit Himself bears witness with our spirit that we are children of God (Romans 8:14-16).

It is by the Spirit that we can call God "*Abba!* Father!" Identity as a child of God is wrapped up with God's Spirit's bearing witness with "our spirit." We might say that the Holy Spirit is like a birth certificate. It is the Father's way of acknowledging His son and giving him identity in the family of God.

The Holy Spirit, who establishes a relationship with the Father, also establishes a bond between all of God's children. Immediately after speaking of someone's becoming a child of God at baptism, Paul affirmed on two occasions how this erases all barriers between the children.

> There is neither Jew nor Greek, there is neither slave nor free man, there is neither male nor female; for you are all one in Christ Jesus (Galatians 3:28).

> For by one Spirit we were all baptized into one body, whether Jews or Greeks, whether slaves or free, and we were all made to drink of one Spirit (1 Corinthians 12:13).

The Holy Spirit is the bond of brotherhood. If we are children of God, we are automatically brothers. If you have a vertical relationship with God, you also must have a horizontal relationship with all of God's children. The same thing that makes you a child of God makes you a brother in God's family.

The tie that binds Christians together is the Holy Spirit. The same Spirit dwells in every child of God. No matter how diverse two Christians might be from another in physical features, backgrounds and status, they are one in the Spirit.

How the Holy Spirit Dwells in a Christian

If the Holy Spirit *does* dwell in a child of God, *how* does He do it? It is at this point that there is much confusion but little evidence.

It is evident that the Holy Spirit does not dwell in a Christian physically. That would be a contradiction. A spirit is non-physical by nature (Luke 24:39). It would be a mistake to try to see, hear or feel the Holy Spirit dwelling in a child of God. His indwelling is spiritual and not subject to physical sense perception.

The doctrine that the Holy Spirit works through the Word of God is a biblical doctrine. The doctrine that the Holy Spirit works through the Word of God only is false.

The Holy Spirit does not dwell in a Christian through the Word of God only. It is true that the Word of God is closely connected with the Holy Spirit. After all, the Holy Spirit inspired those who wrote the Word of God (2 Peter 1:20,21). Things that are attributed to the Holy Spirit are sometimes attributed to the Word of God (refer to Chapter 11).

The Scripture identifies the Word of God as being an instrument of the Holy Spirit. Paul, in describing the

Alive in the Spirit!

Christian armor, identified the Word of God as being the sword of the Spirit: "And take the helmet of salvation, and the sword of the Spirit, which is the word of God" (Ephesians 6:17). The Holy Spirit and the Word of God are no more the same than a soldier is the same thing as his sword. The soldier is the agent. The sword is the instrument he uses. The same can be said of the Holy Spirit and the Word of God. The Holy Spirit is the agent, and the Word of God is the instrument he uses. We can understand why the Scriptures speak of both doing the same thing—they act together as one.

The Holy Spirit, like a soldier, has more than one instrument in his armament. He, like God, can use good and evil men to fulfill His purpose (Romans 9:14-18). He dwells in the church and can use it to accomplish His work (1 Corinthians 3:16; Ephesians 2:22). The way He works in the world is beyond man's comprehension. It is presumptuous to think that we can know all of God's ways. Paul recognized this in his prayer for the Ephesians:

> . . . that He would grant you, according to the riches of His glory; to be strengthened with power through His Spirit in the inner man . . . Now to Him who is able to do exceeding abundantly beyond all that we ask or think, according to the power that works within us (Ephesians 3:16,20).

The prayer Paul prayed for the Ephesians was for the strengthening of power through the Holy Spirit. This power works "within us" and is able to do more than we ask or think.

Certainly, we must acknowledge that the Holy Spirit works through the Word of God. The problem comes if we contend that He works through the Word of God "only."

A basic error of Martin Luther was adding "only" to the doctrine of salvation by faith. He, in reaction to the Roman doctrine of salvation by works only, went to the opposite extreme. Salvation by faith was right. Salvation by faith "only" was false.

Indwelling of the Holy Spirit

The doctrine that the Holy Spirit works through the Word of God is a biblical doctrine. The doctrine that the Holy Spirit works through the Word of God only is false.

The Holy Spirit does not dwell in a Christian as merely a "representative" of God and Christ.

It is true that after the day of Pentecost the role of the Holy Spirit became more prominent than before. He was the Helper whom Jesus sent from the Father to guide the apostles, to empower the church and to dwell in every Christian. God and Christ have not ceased to function in the world (Philippians 2:13; 4:13). They still dwell in the

> *There should be no difficulty in accepting the personal or real indwelling of the Holy Spirit. The Scriptures are plain... God was the giver, and the Holy Spirit was the gift.*

child of God (1 John 4:12; Romans 8:9,10). They still function in response to prayer by helping Christians overcome temptations (1 John 3:22; 1 Corinthians 10:13).

It is also true that it is difficult to separate the person and work of God the Father, God the Son and God the Spirit. Sometimes the Scriptures speak of the Spirit of God. Sometimes they speak of the Spirit of Christ. Sometimes they say the Holy Spirit. Peter identified the "Spirit of Christ" with the Holy Spirit as inspiring the prophets (1 Peter 1:10-12). Paul used the terms "Spirit of God" and "Spirit of Christ" interchangeably in referring to how God dwells in Christians: "However you are not in the flesh but in the Spirit, if indeed the Spirit of God dwells in you. But if anyone does not have the Spirit of Christ he does not belong to Him" (Romans 8:9). This passage demonstrates that the indwelling of the Holy Spirit is not merely the Father and the Son's representative dwelling in a Christian. We do not have to show by some human analogy or reasoned proposition "how" the Spirit dwells in a Christian any more than we have to show "how" God became flesh in Jesus Christ. Both must be believed because the Scriptures affirm them. The wisest theologian, however, cannot discover the "how."

The Holy Spirit does not dwell in a Christian by His teaching and influence only. If that were the case, then an infidel who happened to be a biblical scholar would have the Holy Spirit dwelling in him.

No one can deny that the teachings of one person can have an effect upon another person. There is a word to describe this: "influence." It is not "indwelling." Just saying that "influence" means "indwelling" does not make it so. It is such uncritical definitions of words that lead to confusion and misunderstanding.

It may be true that one person cannot inhabit another person in a physical sense. The indwelling of the Holy Spirit, however, is not physical. He does not take up space nor is He limited by time. He is God.

It was the sin of idolatry that tried to make God in physical forms. Pagans sought to limit God in space by building temples for Him. Pagans sought to limit God to form by forming images. The statement of Paul still applies: "The God who made the world and all things in it, since He is Lord of heaven and earth, does not dwell in temples made with hands; neither is He served by human hands as though He needed anything" (Acts 17:24,25). The nature of God is such that He can dwell in a man if He so desires. He is not limited by physical matter or human limitations. We are really limiting God when we suggest that He can only dwell in man through His influence and teachings.

In the discussion of how the Holy Spirit dwells in a Christian, it is enough to say that He does. The Bible does not reveal all of the philosophical questions surrounding this fact. It is enough to believe it. What we must

Indwelling of the Holy Spirit

avoid is speculation about words that lead to ignorant speculation and division (1 Timothy 6:4; 2 Timothy 2:14,23; Titus 3:9).

The first few centuries after the Word became flesh in Jesus Christ, there was much speculation about "how God became man." Philosophers and theologians get so wrapped up in discussing the "how" that they sometimes forget the fact that He did become man.

Study Questions

1. List three Old Testament predictions of the coming of the Holy Spirit. How and when were they fulfilled?
2. Find New Testament passages showing that God, Christ and the Holy Spirit, all three, dwell in a Christian.
3. Discuss the indwelling of the Holy Spirit as He is described as these:
   - Gift
   - Seal
   - Pledge
   - Mark of identity
4. Is it possible to know all about "how" the Holy Spirit dwells in a Christian? Why?
5. Could one pray today a prayer as Paul did for the Ephesians that the power of the Holy Spirit work in them beyond "all that we ask or think?"
6. What is the relationship between the Holy Spirit and the Word of God?
7. Bring a newspaper clipping to class that shows how some believe that emotional experiences are evidence of God's dwelling in them.
8. Memory work: Ephesians 3:20.

End Notes

[1]See also Romans 8:9-17.

[2]The false doctrine about the Holy Spirit in Calvinism does deny the free will of man, and the false doctrine about the Holy Spirit in Charismatic religion does affirm that He works in a miraculous way today. Neither of these false doctrines is involved in affirming that the Holy Spirit dwells in a child of God. We must not be guilty of reacting so strongly to error on one extreme that we fall into error on the other extreme.

[3]For a fuller discussion see Everett Ferguson, "The Seal of the Covenant," *Firm Foundation* (October 20, 1964), p. 667.

[4]Johannes Behm, "*arrabon*," *The Theological Dictionary of the New Testament* (Grand Rapids: Wm B. Eerdmans, 1964), p. 475.

EIGHT

Spiritual Gifts

Perhaps no aspect of the New Testament teachings about the Holy Spirit is more misunderstood than spiritual gifts. Spiritual gifts are sometimes understood as the baptism of the Holy Spirit or the gift of the Holy Spirit. Spiritual gifts are sometimes understood as human emotional experiences. The result is confusion. One person's use of the term "spiritual gifts" might have little to do with another person's understanding of the term.

This chapter will deal with the definition, the source, the purposes and the possessors of spiritual gifts in the New Testament.

Definition

The word that is translated "spiritual gifts" is *pneumatikos*. It has a broad meaning but three times refers to gifts of a spiritual nature (Romans 1:11; 1 Corinthians 12:1; 14:1). Another word translated "gifts" and often used in the context of spiritual gifts is *charisma* (see Romans 1:11; 1 Corinthians 12:4,9,28,30,31). The basic content of this word is "grace." It refers to a "free gift," one given by grace.

Neither term infers supernatural powers. The emphasis of the former is on the spiritual nature of the gift. The emphasis of the latter is that it is freely given. Both words are used in Paul's introductory statement in Romans: "For I long to see you in order that I may impart some spiritual gift to you, that you may be established" (Romans 1:11). Two things can be learned about spiritual gifts from this passage. First, such gifts were pneumatic in nature and freely given. Second, the presence of Paul had something to do with the Christians in Rome receiving the gifts.

The word *charisma* is used later in Romans to describe grace gifts in the church. None of the seven gifts mentioned demanded any supernatural power.[1] All were God-given, natural gifts.[2] The use of the word in the context of spiritual gifts in 1 Corinthians shows that sometimes it can be associated with supernatural powers.[3]

We must not put special meaning on these words that are not found in the Scriptures. Their use may or may not involve supernatural power. Both of these general terms are used in 1 Corinthians 12 referring to miraculous powers received from the Holy Spirit by Christians in Corinth. This is perhaps the reason that some people might think that these words refer to miraculous powers in other places. We must always understand the meaning of these words in their context.

Miraculous Spiritual Gifts

Miracles in the New Testament seem to have come from three sources. The Holy Spirit was involved in each source. The term "spiritual gifts" is used in only one of these sources.

First, miracles were performed by Jesus. These were confirming miracles. They bore witness to the fact that God was with Him. Nicodemus said, "No one can do these signs that You do unless God is with him" (John 3:2). They showed the people that Jesus, as God, had the power to forgive sins. Jesus indicated this in His statement to the Jewish scribes:

> For which is easier, to say, "Your sins are forgiven," or to say, "Rise and walk"? But in order that you may know that the Son of Man has authority on earth to forgive sins—then He said to the paralytic, "Rise, take up your bed, and go home" (Matthew 9:5,6).

Alive in the Spirit!

Miracles confirmed Him as being the Son of God. John's summary statement about the miracles of Jesus clearly shows their purpose:

> Many other signs therefore Jesus also performed in the presence of the disciples, which are not written in this book; but these have been written that you may believe that Jesus is the Christ, the Son of God; and that believing you may have life in His name (John 20:30,31).

It is not clear what part the Holy Spririt had in these miracles of Jesus. We know that Jesus was born of the Holy Spirit (Luke 1:3,5). The Holy Spirit descended on Him at His baptism (Matthew 3:16,17). Jesus received the Holy Spirit "without measure" (John 3:34). He cast out demons by the Holy Spirit (Matthew 12:28). He gave the Holy Spirit to His disciples (John 20:22). It would be impossible to separate the miracles of Jesus from the work of the Holy Spirit. Perhaps the work of the Holy Spirit in Jesus can best be understood more as the unity of the Godhead rather than some power given to Jesus by the Holy Spirit.

Second, miracles were performed by the apostles. These miracles confirmed their apostolic office. That was the argument Paul made to those who questioned his apostleship.

> ... for in no respect was I inferior to the most eminent apostles, even though I am a nobody. The signs of a true apostle were performed among you with all perseverance, by signs and wonders and miracles (2 Corinthians 12:12. See also Romans 15:17-20).

Miraculous signs confirmed the true apostles as being genuine and distinguished from false apostles (2 Corinthians 11:13-15).

Numerous signs are recorded in Acts, which were worked by the apostles. There were miracles of healings, raising the dead, striking a person blind, casting out

Spiritual Gifts

demons, not being injured by a snake bite and others. None were more distinctive to the apostolic office than the miracle of laying hands on individuals in order for them to receive the Holy Spirit. This could be done only by an apostle. This "laying on of the apostles' hands" gave the recipient supernatural power to work miracles.

The first time such a sign was recorded was in connection with the Christians in Samaria. Luke recorded that when Samaritans "believed Philip preaching the good news about the kingdom of God and the name of Jesus Christ, they were baptized" (Acts 8:12). This made them children of God and caused them to receive the forgiveness of sins and the gift of the Holy Spirit (Acts 2:38). The Holy Spirit that we receive at baptism was not all the Samaritans were to receive. When the apostles in Jerusalem heard about the conversion of the Samaritans, they sent Peter and John to Samaria.

> . . . who came down and prayed for them, that they might receive the Holy Spirit. For He had not yet fallen upon any of them; they had simply been baptized in the name of the Lord Jesus. Then they began laying their hands on them, and they were receiving the Holy Spirit (Acts 8:15-17).

Those who had received the gift of the Holy Spirit at baptism now received the Holy Spirit through the laying on of the apostles' hands. There was a difference. Not all Christians in Samaria received the Holy Spirit through the laying on of the apostles' hands. Luke recorded how Simon, a former sorcerer, wanted to receive this power. He could see that the Holy Spirit was "bestowed through the laying on of the apostles' hands" and offered money to obtain this power (Acts 8:18,19).

Luke recorded other examples of individuals' receiving the "laying on of the apostles' hands." Many of those who received it were able to do supernatural things. The seven men appointed to serve tables in Jerusalem received the laying on of the apostles' hands. Two of them, Stephen and Philip, were able to work miracles later (Acts 6:8; 8:6).

Alive in the Spirit!

The 12 men baptized by Paul at Ephesus were able to speak in tongues and prophesy after Paul, an apostle, laid hands on them (Acts 19:6). Timothy had received "the gift of God" through the laying on of Paul's hands (2 Timothy 1:6).

The apostolic office enabled the apostles to work miracles. These signs confirmed their authenticity. The miracle of the Holy Spirit's being given through the laying on of hands was a unique power possessed only by the apostles.

Several things can be known about this miracle. First, it could be received only through the laying on of the apostles' hands. Second, it involved receiving the Holy Spirit. Third, those who received it had supernatural power to work certain kinds of miracles. Fourth, it was called the gift of God.

It is very probable that the supernatural powers Paul referred to as "spiritual gifts" came about because men received the laying on of the apostles' hands. Those who possessed supernatural spiritual gifts were from churches where apostles had been or were in some way connected with apostles.[4] There is no evidence of such supernatural spiritual gifts in churches where apostles had not been. Since this is the only "unique" miracle performed by the apostles, it could well be one of the "signs of an apostle."

Third, miracles were performed by those who, through the Holy Spirit, possessed spiritual gifts.

It has been shown already that miracles were worked by those who received the "laying on of the apostles' hands." The words "spiritual gifts" are not connected with these miracles. The Scriptures do, however, connect these miracles with the reception of the Holy Spirit.

Three basic passages are usually connected with spiritual gifts. Only one passage connects these spiritual gifts to the Holy Spirit. Only one passage involves miraculous signs of confirmation.

The first passage contains a list of non-miraculous *charisma* gifts. Paul wrote a letter to Rome in which he expressed a desire to be with them that he might give them a spiritual gift: "For I long to see you in order that

Spiritual Gifts

I may impart some spiritual gift to you, that you may be established" (Romans 1:11).[5] Paul recognized that they did not possess "spiritual gifts," even though he would later speak of them having "grace gifts." He, as an apostle, could bestow "spiritual gifts" upon them when he came to Rome.

In the context of showing that the body should be united, even though different members have different functions, Paul exhorted Christians to exercise their different "grace gifts" for the good of the whole church.

> And since we have gifts that differ according to the grace given to us, let each exercise them accordingly; if prophecy, according to the proportion of his faith; if service, in his serving; or he who teaches, in his teaching; or he who exhorts, in his exhortation; he who gives, with liberality; he who leads, with diligence; he who shows mercy, with cheerfulness (Romans 12:6-8).

Several things should be noted in this passage. First, the gift mentioned is a "grace" gift not a "spiritual" gift. Second, none of the seven gifts mentioned are uniquely miraculous in their nature. Third, the Holy Spirit is not connected with any of the gifts.

This passage is not talking about miraculous spiritual gifts given by the Holy Spirit, but natural gifts that different individual Christians possess, which were to be unselfishly used for the whole church.

The second passage also recognizes the diversity of gifts that are found in the church and exhorts that they be used to benefit the whole church.

> But to each one of us grace was given according to the measure of Christ's gift. Therefore it says, "When He ascended on high, He led captive a host of captives, and He gave gifts to men" . . . And He gave some as apostles, and some as prophets, and some as evangelists, and some as pastors and teachers, for the equipping of the saints for the work of service, to the building up of the body of Christ (Ephesians 4:7,8,11,12).[6]

Alive in the Spirit!

Several things should be noted about this passage in connection with the understanding of miraculous spiritual gifts.

First, neither of the words "grace gift" or "spiritual gift" are used in the passage. (The word *doma* is used.) The passage does indicate that gifts were given by grace, even though the technical word is not used.

Second, the Holy Spirit is not referred to in the passage. The giver of the gifts is Christ. The meaning is not that Christ is distributing miraculous spiritual gifts, but that Christ is maturing His church through the different offices of apostles, prophets, evangelists and teaching pastors. Each function is designed for "building up the body of Christ." Miraculous spiritual gifts might be involved. The Holy Spirit might be active in giving such gifts. The text, however, does not indicate that.

Third, the passage is not referring to the cessation of spiritual gifts but the maturing of the body of Christ. Other passages show that miraculous spiritual gifts will cease with maturity (1 Corinthians 13:8-13), but such is not the teaching of this text.

The third passage contains the basic teachings about miraculous spiritual gifts. Both the words for "grace gifts" and "spiritual gifts" are used in the text. Many of the gifts enumerated in the text are miraculous in their nature. The source of these gifts is the Holy Spirit. These gifts were possessed by Christians in a church where an apostle had spent more than one and a half years.

A background of the passage is found in the first chapter of the book:

> I thank my God always concerning you, for the grace of God which was given you in Christ Jesus, that in everything you were enriched in Him, in all speech and all knowledge, even as the testimony concerning Christ was confirmed in you, so that you are not lacking in any gift. . . . (1 Corinthians 1:4-7).

The passage uses *charisma* for the gifts that were given by God. Such gifts were possessed by the Corinthians in

Spiritual Gifts

abundance. They were lacking in no gift. They were enriched in everything. Two of the gifts, speech and knowledge, are mentioned. They are among the spiritual gifts listed later in the epistle.

Two lists of spiritual gifts were given by Paul in 1 Corinthians 12. In these lists are both kinds of gifts—those which are miraculous by nature and those which are from the natural endowment of men. They are listed together. Perhaps the naturally endowed gifts are listed because they were enhanced by the Holy Spirit in a miraculous way at Corinth. The two kinds of gifts are listed side by side here for comparison.

1 Corinthians 12:8-10	1 Corinthians 12:28-30
Word of wisdom	
Word of knowledge	
Faith	
Gifts of healing	Gifts of healing
Effecting of miracles	Miracles
Prophecy	
Distinguishing of spirit	
Various kinds of tongues	Various kinds of tongues
Interpretation of tongues	Interpretation of tongues
	Apostles
	Prophets
	Teachers
	Administrations
	Helps

There are 14 spiritual gifts to be found in both lists. Four of the more spectacular gifts are found in both lists and are miraculous in their nature. Most of the gifts are not miraculous by nature, but individuals could have received a miraculous enhancing of these natural gifts. The three gifts—apostles, prophets and teachers—are gifts of office and are to be compared to the similar list in Ephesians listed earlier.

The most complete list of spiritual gifts, along with their source and purpose, is given by Paul at the beginning of his discussion about the abuse of these gifts at Corinth.

Alive in the Spirit!

> Now concerning spiritual gifts . . . Now there are varieties of gifts, but the same **Spirit**. And there are varieties of ministries, and the same Lord. And there are varieties of effects, but the same God who works all things in all persons. But to each one is given the manifestation of the **Spirit** for the common good. For to one is given the word of wisdom through the **Spirit**, and to another the word of knowledge according to the same **Spirit**; to another faith by the same **Spirit**, and to another gifts of healing by the one **Spirit**, and to another the effecting of miracles, and to another prophecy and to another the distinguishing of spirits, to another various kinds of tongues, and to another the interpretation of tongues. But one in the same **Spirit** works all things, distributing to each one individually just as He wills (1 Corinthians 12:1,4-11).

Six times in the text the Holy Spirit is shown to be the source of these spiritual gifts. The gifts are for the common good of the church. The gifts do not come from the seeking of the person but from the will of the Spirit.

Paul devoted chapters 12-14 to the discussion of spiritual gifts where several instructions are given to the Corinthian Christians.

First, these gifts were useful in the church then, and the greater gifts were to be desired by Christians (12:31).

Second, a more excellent way was predicted by Paul at which time such gifts as miraculous knowledge, prophecy and tongues would cease as the church grew to maturity (13:8-13).[7]

Third, such spiritual gifts were useless without love (13:1-7,13). These gifts will not save an individual and are useless in edifying the church without love. The gifts will pass away, but faith, hope and love will continue to abide in the church.

Fourth, the gift of tongues is inferior to prophecy because it cannot edify the church without being interpreted (14:1-19). Its abuse is a sign of immaturity, and its use in the assembly is strictly regulated (14:20-40).

Spiritual Gifts

Purposes of Miraculous Spiritual Gifts

The first purpose of miraculous spiritual gifts from the Holy Spirit is the same as any other New Testament miracle—to confirm the man and/or his message as being from God.[8] This is evident because of the confirming nature of the miracles performed by Stephen and Philip (Acts 6:8-10; 8:6,7). This confirmation purpose is reflected in the statement made in Hebrews:

> ... how shall we escape if we neglect so great salvation? After it was at the first spoken through the Lord, it was confirmed to us by those who heard, God also bearing witness with them, both by signs and wonders and by various miracles and by gifts of the Holy Spirit according to His own will (Hebrews 2:3-4).

The gifts of the Holy Spirit are listed as confirming signs along with other "signs, wonders and miracles."

A second purpose of the miraculous spiritual gifts from the Holy Spirit is for edifying the church. As already noted, both the non-miraculous and miraculous grace gifts mentioned in the epistles are for the "building up of the body."

> And since we have gifts that differ according to the grace given to us, let each exercise them accordingly (Romans 12:6).

> But to each one is given the manifestation of the Spirit for the common good (1 Corinthians 12:7).

> And He gave some as apostles, and some as prophets, and some as evangelists, and some as pastors and teachers, for the equipping of the saints for the work of service, to the building up of the body of Christ (Ephesians 4:11,12).

At the beginning of the church, there were no New Testament Scriptures to give directions in faith and conduct. God's will could be discerned only by inspired men. The inspired apostles could not be everywhere; so others were given the gifts of prophecy, knowledge and wisdom by which the church could reach maturity. It was the abuse of the edifying purpose of these gifts that Paul sought to correct at Corinth. Two exhortations at the close of his discussion of spiritual gifts express this idea. "Let all things be done for edification" (1 Corinthians 12:26), and "Let all things be done properly and in an orderly manner" (1 Corinthians 12:40).

Spiritual gifts were present in the early church for the purpose of confirmation and edification. They were grace gifts and came from the Holy Spirit. They were to pass away as their need diminished. They were helpful in supplying guidance in the infancy of the church before the full revelation of the will of God in the New Testament.

Study Questions

1. Discuss the difference between the terms "spiritual gift" *(pneumatikos)* and "grace gift" *(charisma)*.
2. In what way were the grace gifts at Rome different from those at Corinth?
3. What practical lesson can be learned from the diversity/unity of both miraculous and non-miraculous grace gifts?
4. What is the possible connection between miraculous spiritual gifts and "the laying on of the apostles' hands?"
5. List the 14 spiritual gifts found in 1 Corinthians 12.
6. Discuss miraculous spiritual gifts as to their . . .
    - Nature
    - Purposes
    - Source
    - End
7. Discuss 1 Corinthians 12:12-31 as it relates to the use of spiritual gifts.
8. Memory work: Romans 12:6.

End Notes

[1] Romans 12:6-8. The gifts were prophecy, service, teaching, exhorting, giving, leading and showing mercy.

[2] It should be noted that the Holy Spirit is not referred to in the *charisma* gifts in Romans, which were natural gifts. He is often connected with the *charisma* gifts in 1 Corinthians.

[3] 1 Corinthians 12 uses the word several times. Included are such gifts

Spiritual Gifts

as healing, miracles, distinguishing of spirits, tongues and interpretation of tongues.

[4] See Chapters 6 and 8 which show that Corinth had miraculous spiritual gifts, and Rome did not. It was, no doubt, because of the presence of an apostle at Corinth and the absence of an apostle at Rome.

[5] Note: Both *charisma* and *pneumatikos* are in this text.

[6] The quotation is from Psalm 68:18 and reads that gifts were "received" rather than "given." Both the Hebrew and the LXX support such a reading.

[7] See Jimmy Jividen, *Glossolalia* (Fort Worth: Star Bible, 1971), pp. 116-128 for a full discussion of this passage.

[8] See Jimmy Jividen, *Miracles, From God or Man* (Abilene: ACU Press, 1988), pp. 78-86.

NINE

Blasphemy Against the Holy Spirit

The blasphemy against the Holy Spirit is mentioned in only three places in the Scriptures. Confusion about this teaching, like the baptism of the Holy Spirit, does not exist so much because of what the Scriptures *say* as it does about theories that men have devised *about* it.

Some live in terror of accidentally or through deception by the devil's uttering words that will cause them to be eternally damned. Others live in hopeless despair of having already committed the unpardonable sin of blaspheming the Holy Spirit and, therefore, must live their lives beyond the reach of the grace of God. Such beliefs have been promoted by either ignorant or deceitful religious leaders who use such a doctrine as a means of controlling their followers.

Definitions

The word blasphemy means "evil speaking" generally. It can be either against God or man. It is used with reference to the reviling the Jews did against Paul and Barnabas in Antioch (Acts 13:45; 18:6). It is translated "slander" when referring to the malicious speech that comes from the heart of man (Matthew 15:19; Mark 7:22; Colossians 3:8). In a religious context it refers to "impious and irreverent speech against God." It refers to the verbalization of what is already in the heart of a man who utters it.

Two Old Testament passages are behind Jesus' reference to the blasphemy against the Holy Spirit. They show both

Blasphemy Against the Holy Spirit

the attitude that brings about blasphemy and the penalty God demanded for blasphemy in the Old Testament.

The first passage is in a context of showing the difference between intentional and unintentional sins. The intentional sin is called blasphemy.

> You shall have one law for him who does anything unintentionally, for him who is native among the sons of Israel and for the alien who sojourns among them. But the person who does anything defiantly, whether he is native or an alien, that one is blaspheming the Lord; and that person shall be cut off from among his people. Because he has despised the word of the Lord and has broken His commandment, that person shall be completely cut off; his guilt shall be on him (Numbers 15:29-31).

Defiantly disobeying God's commandments is regarded as blasphemy. One who does so is to be cut off from God's people because he "despised the word of the Lord."

Blasphemy was a grievous sin which was not tolerated by Israel. The drastic punishment of stoning was given to the son of a Danite woman who had blasphemed the Name and cursed. The law of Moses was plain: ". . . the one who blasphemes the name of the Lord shall surely be put to death; all the congregation shall certainly stone him" (Leviticus 24:16). The name of the Lord is Holy, and it is not to be profaned by man. Under Moses' law there did not seem to be any room for repentance or the opportunity of restoration to the favor of God and His people.

Three Passages

Each of the synoptic gospels gives the teachings of Jesus concerning blaspheming against the Holy Spirit. Matthew and Mark have identical context.

Jesus had cast a demon out of a blind, dumb man and healed him. The scribes and Pharisees could not deny the miracle but charged that its source was Beelzebub. They

Alive in the Spirit!

said, "This man casts out demons only by Beelzebub the ruler of demons" (Matthew 12:24).

Jesus responded to them by showing two reasons why that was impossible. First, it would mean that Satan was fighting against himself. This would be illogical and self-destructive. Second, it would also infer that the "sons" of the Pharisees who claimed to cast out demons were also casting out demons by Beelzebub.

Jesus then gave them two warnings. First, since He cast out demons by the Spirit of God, it was evident that the kingdom of God had come. Second, speaking evil of the Holy Spirit by whom Jesus had cast out the demon was a sin for which there was no forgiveness.

> Therefore I say to you, any sin and blasphemy shall be forgiven men; but blasphemy against the Spirit shall not be forgiven. And whoever shall speak a word against the Son of Man, it shall be forgiven him; but whoever shall speak against the Holy Spirit, it shall not be forgiven him, either in this age, or in the age to come (Matthew 12:31,32).[1]

The passage shows that blasphemy against the Holy Spirit is more serious than other sins, even blasphemy against the Son of Man. It has eternal consequences because it cannot be forgiven.

The similar passage in Luke is in another setting. The context is also a response to the hostile questioning of the scribes and Pharisees. There is nothing, however, about casting out a demon. There is, rather, a group of warnings that Jesus gave His disciples about the opposition of the Pharisees (Luke 11:53,54).

First, there was a warning to beware of the leaven of the Pharisees, which was hypocrisy. Jesus said the hypocrisy would ultimately be exposed (Luke 12:1-3). Second, there was a warning not to be afraid of persecution—those who would kill the body—because they were not forgotten by God who cared for even the sparrows (Luke 12:4-7). Third, there was a warning not to deny the Son of Man lest He deny them before the angels of God (Luke 12:8,9).

Blasphemy Against the Holy Spirit

Fourth, there is a warning about blasphemy against the Holy Spirit because it is an unforgivable sin: "And everyone who will speak a word against the Son of Man, it shall be forgiven him; but he who blasphemes against the Holy Spirit, it shall not be forgiven him" (Luke 12:10). The language of these passages does not identify clearly the nature of the blasphemy against the Holy Spirit. We must look to the context.

The context of all three passages deals with the opposition of the scribes and Pharisees to Jesus. They were plotting against Him. They were denying that the Holy Spirit was the power through which He cast out demons.

Our understanding of the blasphemy of the Holy Spirit must fit into this context. The easiest explanation is that the blasphemy against the Holy Spirit is attributing the work of the Holy Spirit to Beelzebub.[2]

This understanding certainly would be speaking against the Holy Spirit. It would be saying that He was evil, and His motives were deceitful.

This understanding would make it more serious than blasphemy against the Son of Man. Three thousand on the day of Pentecost were baptized for the remission of sins, even though they had denied Jesus and delivered

---

God's grace is sufficient to cover every sin for which a man can repent.

Him up to Pilate. They were forgiven because they came to believe through the "witness of the Holy Spirit" (Acts 2:33). If that same group had attributed the work of the Holy Spirit on the day of Pentecost to the Devil, they would have never received the forgiveness of sins. By attributing the power of the Holy Spirit to the devil, they would have rejected the only means by which they could have come to faith.

This understanding would fit a statement which Paul was later to make about rejecting truth.

> . . . because they did not receive the love of the truth so as to be saved. And for this reason God will send upon them a deluding influence so that they might believe what is false, in order that they all may be judged who did not believe the truth, but took pleasure in wickedness (2 Thessalonians 2:9-12).

Those who reject what truth they have will ultimately be blinded and unable to receive any other truth. The vacuum of their soul will breed deception, and that deception will ultimately lead to their damnation. Because the Pharisees did not want to believe Jesus, they deceived themselves into thinking that His miracles were of the devil.

This understanding would fit the Old Testament background, which identifies blasphemy as a defiant and willful sin and makes it punishable by death.

Complementary Passages

Three other New Testament passages speak of men sinning in such a way that they find themselves beyond forgiveness.

Two of these passages are in Hebrews. They are different from those passages in the Gospels that speak of the blasphemy against the Holy Spirit. Instead of rejecting Jesus by attributing His power to the devil, those addressed in Hebrews were former disciples of Jesus who had willfully gone into total apostasy. Instead of rejecting the Holy Spirit who bore witness to Jesus through miracles, those addressed in Hebrews rejected the Holy Spirit who dwelt in them as Christians. Instead of rejecting Jesus, those addressed in Hebrews had forsaken Jesus.

> For in the case of those who have once been enlightened and have tasted of the heavenly gift and have been made partakers of the Holy Spirit, and have

Blasphemy Against the Holy Spirit

> tasted the good word of God and the powers of the age to come, and then have fallen away, it is impossible to renew them again to repentance, since they again crucify to themselves the Son of God, and put Him to open shame (Hebrews 6:4-6).

> For if we go on sinning willfully after receiving the knowledge of the truth, there no longer remains a sacrifice for sins, but a certain terrifying expectation of judgment, and the fury of a fire which will consume the adversaries. Anyone who has set aside the Law of Moses dies without mercy on the testimony of two or three witnesses. How much severer punishment do you think he will deserve who has trampled under foot the Son of God, and has regarded as unclean the blood of the covenant, by which he was sanctified, and has insulted the Spirit of grace? (Hebrews 10:26-29).

Both of these passages are addressed to those who one time knew forgiveness and the power of the Holy Spirit in their lives. Both of these passages show that the Holy Spirit had been rejected by "falling away" or "willful sin." Both of these passages show that it is impossible to recall such individuals to repentance.

Peter also warns of the danger of apostasy as being even worse than the condition of one who is not a Christian.

> For if after they have escaped the defilements of the world by the knowledge of the Lord and Savior Jesus Christ, they are again entangled in them and are overcome, the last state has become worse for them than the first. For it would be better for them not to have known the way of righteousness, than having known it, to turn away from the holy commandment delivered to them. It has happened to them according to the true proverb, "A dog returns to its own vomit" and "A sow, after washing, returns to wallowing in the mire" (2 Peter 2:20-22).

It is more difficult for a believer to return from his apostasy than it is for an unbeliever to come to faith in Jesus Christ.

Alive in the Spirit!

There is a point in apostasy in which there is no longer a will to repent.[3]

We must avoid the temptation to equate the Scriptures that speak of the blasphemy against the Holy Spirit with those that speak of believers going into total apostasy. In three ways they *are* alike. Both speak of the impossibility of forgiveness. Both speak of the rejection of the Holy Spirit. Both will lead to eternal damnation.

In other ways they are different. The sins were different. One was initial rejection, and the other was total apostasy. Those who sinned were different. One rejected Him, and the other forsook Him.

Blasphemy against the Holy Spirit is attributing the power of the Holy Spirit to Beelzebub. It is a rejection of Him who bears witness to the Son of God and, therefore, makes it impossible for someone to come to faith. That person will never be forgiven for this because he has cut off the means by which faith can come.

Total apostasy is brought about by "falling away" and committing "willful sin." In this state a person has "crucified and shamed Christ" and "insulted the Spirit of grace." Such a hardened heart cannot come to repentance.

Conclusions

There are currently a number of misconceptions about the blasphemy against the Holy Spirit. In some cases it has led to terror because someone believed he had committed such a sin and could not possibly be saved. In other cases it has led to hardened indifference. There is no use trying if grace is denied by God, and there is no forgiveness. In other cases someone is almost afraid to talk about the Holy Spirit lest he say something that would be blasphemy against Him.

We must not understand the blasphemy of the Holy Spirit to be the rejection of contemporary miraculous claims. We reject contemporary miraculous claims because the Scriptures warn of false prophets working false signs to deceive.[4] It is the Holy Spirit's work through the

Blasphemy Against the Holy Spirit

Scriptures that provides the means of testing the prophets and the signs they claim. Exposing false miracles is not against the Holy Spirit.

Claiming miracles that are not really New Testament miracles *is* against the Holy Spirit. We must not confuse God's orderly work in the world with the miraculous signs of the New Testament. It is a sin to attribute the deception of men to the power of the Holy Spirit.

We must not connect the blasphemy of the Holy Spirit with sins in the past that are so terrible that we might think them to be unpardonable. The fact that one is able to feel guilty about such sins is evidence that he is not

> *If man's will refuses to bend in repentance, then God's will refuses to bend in forgiveness. It is not that God refuses grace; it is that those who blaspheme against the Holy Spirit have hardened their* **heart** *beyond repentance.*

beyond the grace of God. If an unpardonable sin had been committed, then we would not feel guilty. We, like the Pharisees Jesus reproved, would twist the facts to fit what we wanted to believe. The ability to feel guilt is from God. Such guilt can lead to repentance. God's grace is sufficient to cover every sin for which a man can repent. A person who has blasphemed the name of Christ can be forgiven. Saul was (1 Timothy 1:12-15). One who has lived as an immoral reprobate can be forgiven. The Corinthians were (1 Corinthians 6:9-11). One who doubted the resurrection of Jesus can be forgiven. Thomas was (John 20:24-29). One who has been guilty of crucifying Jesus Christ can be forgiven. Three thousand who were guilty

Alive in the Spirit!

of crucifying Christ were forgiven on the day of Pentecost (Acts 2:23,38,41).

We must not see in God's judgment against those who blaspheme against the Holy Spirit a limitation of the grace of God. Not only is the will of God involved in extending forgiveness, the will of man is also involved. If man's will refuses to bend in repentance, then God's will refuses to bend in forgiveness. It is not that God refuses grace; it is that those who blaspheme against the Holy Spirit have hardened their heart *beyond* repentance.

The blasphemy against the Holy Spirit is identified in the New Testament as being the Pharisees attributing the power by which Jesus worked miracles to Beelzebub instead of the Holy Spirit. In a technical sense it cannot be committed today because Jesus is not physically present in the world.

We might draw an analogy of something that would be similar to the sin of blasphemy against the Holy Spirit. If a person today heard the Gospel of Jesus Christ, along with the many miracles that are recorded in Scriptures, and chose not to believe, but willfully rejected it, he would be a willful unbeliever.

If, in his own self-delusion, he would claim that the Gospel was not from God, but of the devil, he would have no desire to believe it. If he were to affirm that the Scriptures were not inspired of the Holy Spirit, but were the work of Satan, he would disregard their authority. If he were to declare that Jesus was not the Christ, but merely a deluded man who falsely claimed to be divine, then there would be no motive to follow Him. Such a man hardly could be forgiven. He has cut off any avenue to produce faith. He has rejected any criteria by which he could be convicted of sin. His deluded mind is programed to resist any knowledge of truth.

Such would not, in a technical sense, be the blasphemy against the Holy Spirit, yet it shows how a similar rejection of God's power today can lead us outside the realm of grace. It is not the unwillingness of God to extend grace that causes one who has so rejected Him to be without

Blasphemy Against the Holy Spirit

forgiveness. It is man's willful rebellion. Such rebellion cuts off all roads to either knowing God or receiving His mercy.

Study Questions

1. What was the blasphemy against the Holy Spirit? Is it possible to commit such a sin today?
2. Why is the blasphemy against the Holy Spirit unforgivable?
3. What is the difference between willful unbelief and total apostasy?
4. How is apostasy a sin against the Holy Spirit?
5. How is apostasy a more serious sin than never knowing about Jesus Christ?
6. How is total apostasy similar to blasphemy against the Holy Spirit?
7. What makes any sin beyond the grace of God?
8. Memory work: Mark 3:29.

End Notes

[1] Mark 3:28,29 is a briefer parallel passage. The basic difference is that Mark called the sin an "eternal sin."

[2] Justifying sin by calling it good was not a new thing. Isaiah tells of those who "call evil good, and good evil." See Isaiah 5:20.

[3] See 1 John 5:16-17. There is no doubt some connection between this and the "sin unto death." One is not even to pray for one who sins a sin unto death.

[4] Matthew 7:21,22; 24:23-26; 2 Thessalonians 2:9-11; 2 Corinthians 11:13-15; 1 Timothy 4:1,2; 1 John 4:1-4.

SECTION THREE

The Present Work of the Holy Spirit

The Holy Spirit did not die with the last of the apostles. He is still alive and well in the world today. His work changed from the confirming miraculous phase during the ministry of Jesus and the apostles to a different phase that will continue until Jesus comes again. The change of His work did not bring about the demise of His person.

In an allegorical sense, we can divide history into three ages: the age of the Father, the age of the Son, and, finally, the age of the Holy Spirit.

God acted in creation, through the patriarchs and prophets and in the history of Israel. Little was said about the Word or the Spirit. This might be called the age of the Father.

The Son acted in the next period. From His birth in Bethlehem of Judea to His resurrection from the dead, Jesus was predominate in God's work among men. Less was said about the Father and the Spirit. This might be called the age of the Son.

The Holy Spirit is acting now. From the day of Pentecost until Jesus comes again, the Holy Spirit has worked powerfully in the world. He is "front and center" in the establishment and growth of the church in Acts. He is the theological basis of much that is taught in the epistles. He still works in the lives of children of God. This might be called the age of the Holy Spirit.

These three divisions are arbitrary. Nowhere in the Scriptures are they listed in this way. They merely reflect how the Scriptures express the activities of the Father, the Son and the Holy Spirit.

The Present Work of the Holy Spirit

Certainly, this division does not exclude all three personalities of the Godhead working in all ages. In the age of the Father, promise and prophecy pointed to the coming Messiah. In the age of the Son, promise and prophecy pointed to the coming of the Holy Spirit. All of these ages have the Father, Son and the Holy Spirit working in divine unison.

The last age, the age of the Holy Spirit, is of primary interest because that is the age in which we now live.

In this section, we will see that the present work of the Holy Spirit is distinctive from His work in the apostolic period in its nature, its purpose and its scope. The following chart suggests some of these differences.

Work of the Holy Spirit		
	Age of the Apostles	**Today**
Nature	Miraculous	Orderly
Purpose	Confirm man and message	Help and Comfort
Scope	Apostles and those empowered	All children of God

The Holy Spirit works in a different way than He did when He bore witness to Jesus during His personal ministry. Jesus has been confirmed as being the Son of God with the power of the Holy Spirit. This confirmation is recorded in Scripture. This phase of the work of the Holy Spirit has been completed.

The Holy Spirit works in a different way from the way He did when he confirmed the authority of the apostles and inspired those on whom the apostles laid their hands. The Scriptures which He inspired men to write completed this phase of His work.

The present phase of the work of the Holy Spirit is just as important as any other phase of His work. It is different. He now works according to God's will in creation as

> *The Holy Spirit did not die with the last of the apostles. He is still alive and well in the world today. His work changed from the confirming miraculous phase during the ministry of Jesus and the apostles to a different phase that will continue until Jesus comes again. The change of His work did not bring about the demise of His person.*

revealed in the laws of nature. He now works according to God's will in Revelation as revealed in the teaching of the Scriptures. His work is orderly, consistent and harmonious. He works powerfully, but within the limits of the divine laws of creation and revelation.

---TEN---

His Work in Conversion

The work of the Holy Spirit in conversion was the focus of most of the discussion about the Holy Spirit during the last century. Following the teaching of Calvin, and before him Augustine, most of Protestantism believed that there must be a "direct operation of the Holy Spirit" upon a sinner before he could be saved. This doctrine is reflected in the evangelistic practices of most of the religious groups of this time. The "mourner's bench" experience was an expected norm. Those seeking conversion were told to "hit the sawdust trail" and "pray through." Under conviction of sin, they would wait for an emotional experience, which they were told was the coming of the Holy Spirit.

The theological meaning behind this process was rooted in Calvinism, which taught that man was predestined to be either saved or lost by a sovereign God. Nothing he could do would cause him to be saved if he were not among the "elect."

The soul who sought salvation could only wait for the work of God in his life. This, they believed, was an emotional experience that was sometimes accompanied with "spiritual exercises." Such an experience would give assurance of salvation and guarantee that the person would never be lost. The testimonies about this emotional experience that were given in evangelistic meetings gave assurance to the one testifying and encouragement to others to seek similar experiences.

The Holy Spirit was said to be the source of these emotional experiences and automatic actions. The Holy

Spirit was thought to be something "better felt than told." Receiving an experience was evidence of salvation and the presence of the Holy Spirit.

It was no wonder that students of the Scriptures and reasonable men saw such doctrines as false and such experiences as mere emotional excitement.[1] Some people reacted to this "direct operation of the Holy Spirit" in conversion and went to the other extreme of denying that the Holy Spirit had any work in the world at all. They sought to refute the false teaching of the direct operation of the Holy Spirit by saying He did not work at all.

Instead of showing that such emotional experiences and spiritual exercises were not from the Holy Spirit but of human origin, they ended up denying much of what the Holy Spirit does do. In some writings of that time the reader would think that the Holy Spirit should be put in a box and shipped back to the first century where He belonged. In other writings of that time one would think that the Holy Spirit was imprisoned in the Bible and was forbidden to have free course in the world.[2]

The Holy Spirit and Conversion

The Holy Spirit does work in conversion. This cannot be questioned by any careful student of the Scriptures. The problem comes when human experience and paranormal happenings are attributed to the work of the Holy Spirit. These are the devil's counterfeits. Pagan religions of every age have tried to identify the emotional experiences of men with the indwelling of their gods.

If one can identify "how" the Holy Spirit works in conversion in an orderly way, this will show that the experiential claims about the Holy Spirit are false.

The Holy Spirit works in conversion through His work of inspiring those who wrote the Scriptures (2 Peter 1:20-21). We can know that "thy word is truth" (John 17:17) because the Holy Spirit guided them into all truth (John 16:13). Just as Peter spoke on the day of Pentecost "as the Spirit was giving them utterance" (Acts 2:4), so men today

His Work in Conversion

are able to speak the truth of the Scriptures because it was inspired by the Spirit.

Jesus gave a parable of the sower to show the work of the Word of God in conversion (Luke 8:4-15). The field represents the hearts of men. The seed is the Word of God. A new plant is generated when the seed is received into the heart of man. This is the process of conversion. The seed of the kingdom, the Word of God, falls into good and honest hearts. This makes a Christian. We cannot take the work of the Holy Spirit out of the Word which He inspired.

In this way the Holy Spirit works through the Word of God in begetting a child of God. This is the beginning of

---

The Holy Spirit is involved in the new birth as much as the water of baptism. The physical element of water and the power of the Holy Spirit combine to bring about the new birth.

---

the new birth: ". . . for you have been born again not of seed which is perishable but imperishable, that is, through the living and abiding word of God" (1 Peter 1:23).[3] We cannot remove the Holy Spirit from conversion any more than we can remove the vitality of a seed from the generation of a new plant.

The begetting process of the Word of God is expressed by Jesus in His promise of the Holy Spirit. The coming Holy Spirit was to "convict the world concerning sin, and righteousness, and judgment" (John 16:8).[4] The coming Holy Spirit was to bear witness of Christ (John 15:26). The coming Holy Spirit was to guide "into all the truth" and "teach you all things" (John 16:13; 14:26). What the Holy

Alive in the Spirit!

Spirit was to do, the New Testament said was done when the Word of God was preached. The Holy Spirit does the same today when the Word of God is preached.

The Holy Spirit works in conversion through the new birth itself. Jesus' answer to Nicodemus shows the work of the Holy Spirit is involved in the regeneration that takes place at baptism.

> Jesus answered and said to him, Truly, truly, I say to you, unless one is born again he cannot see the kingdom of God . . . unless one is born of water and the Spirit, he cannot enter into the kingdom of God (see John 3:3,5).

The Holy Spirit is involved in the new birth as much as the water of baptism. The physical element of water and the power of the Holy Spirit combine to bring about the new birth.

This seems to be a part of the meaning of Paul's statement to the Corinthians about their baptism: "For by[5] one Spirit we were all baptized into one body" (1 Corinthians 12:13). The Holy Spirit is involved when one is baptized into Christ. He cannot be the physical element of the new birth since He is by very nature a spirit. Just as water is the physical element, the Holy Spirit is the spiritual power of the new birth.

The Holy Spirit works in conversion as God's gift, God's pledge and God's seal to His new child. All three terms are used to refer to the indwelling of the Holy Spirit. As we have discussed earlier, the Holy Spirit is God's gift to His child at baptism. The Holy Spirit is God's seal of the New Covenant that God has made with His people just as circumcision was the seal of the Old Covenant between God and the Jews. The Holy Spirit is a pledge or earnest that God has given, which carries with it a promise of something bigger and better to come. Notice the following brief statements which affirm this:

> . . . and you shall receive the gift of the Holy Spirit (Acts 2:38).

His Work in Conversion

> . . . the Holy Spirit, whom God has given to those who obey Him (Acts 5:32).
>
> . . . and we were all made to drink of one Spirit (1 Corinthians 12:13).
>
> . . . God sent forth the Spirit of His Son into our hearts (Galatians 4:6).
>
> . . . you were sealed in Him with the Holy Spirit of promise (Ephesians 1:13).
>
> . . . the Holy Spirit of God, by whom you were sealed (Ephesians 4:30).
>
> . . . God gave to us the Spirit as a pledge (2 Corinthians 5:5).[6]

The Holy Spirit who dwells in the Christian gives him identity as God's child and makes him a brother or sister to all of God's children. The Holy Spirit is received when one is baptized into Christ. The Holy Spirit is a part of his new creaturehood.

Errors About the Holy Spirit in Conversion

Many of the things that have been taught about the Holy Spirit in conversion are without Scriptural evidence and must be rejected. These doctrines have grown out of two basic misconceptions of the nature and work of the Holy Spirit.

The first error is that the possession of and/or the work of the Holy Spirit is identified with a human emotional experience. Emotional experiences change with time and often contradict the experiences of others. Such subjective emotions cannot be evidence of the Holy Spirit. The difference between an ordinary human experience and what is claimed as a supernatural spiritual experience is not in its content. It is in its interpretation. Any common, everyday happening can be interpreted as a religious experience and made to confirm what one wants to believe.

This is not to negate the importance of experience in the Christian life; it is to show that experiences cannot be the criteria for knowing God or understanding His will.

Alive in the Spirit!

The second error is that the Holy Spirit is thought to be so far removed from man and the world that we can expect Him to work through the Word of God only. This view of the Holy Spirit is a denial of the immanent working of God in the world.

The Conversion Experience and the Holy Spirit

The experiential view of the Holy Spirit is as old as the New Testament itself. We can see it reflected in some of the false teachings refuted in the Scriptures.

It was probably an experiential view of the Holy Spirit that was behind some of the abuse of the spiritual gifts at Corinth. Some Christians at Corinth were confusing irrational excitement with genuine miraculous gifts of the Holy Spirit. Paul showed the similarities of the Corinthian practices with the experiential religions of the pagan cults: "You know that when you were pagans, you were led astray to the dumb idols, however you were led" (1 Corinthians 12:2). Like the pagans, these Corinthians were not concerned with the rational understanding of what they were doing. They were concerned only with the experience.

It was probably an experiential view of the Holy Spirit that was behind the "pre-gnostic error"[7] refuted by John. It would appear that the false teachers John refuted believed in a dualism that understood matter as evil and spirit as good. This resulted in anything involved with matter being on a lower and less important level than the spiritual realm in which they thought they lived. Physical commands of the Lord were unimportant and could be ignored. The practice of brotherly love and benevolence were unnecessary and had nothing to do with one's relationship with God. This doctrine was grounded in the view that a person had an intuitive spiritual relationship with God through experience. This relationship had nothing to do with the Word of God, commandment keeping, benevolence and brotherly love. John clearly shows this was not the case.

His Work in Conversion

> And by this we know that we have come to know Him, if we keep His commandments. The one who says, "I have come to know Him," and does not keep His commandments, is a liar and the truth is not in him; but whoever keeps His word, in him the love of God has truly been perfected. By this we know that we are in Him (1 John 2:3-5).

The way to know God is not through human emotional experiences, but through yielding your will to God in obeying His commandments. Subjective emotional feelings are inadequate. Assurance can only be found in the objective reality of humble obedience.

The experiential view of the Holy Spirit can be found in a number of groups throughout church history. The one which perhaps has had the greatest influence on the western Protestant world was Calvinism. Calvin understood that one must have a personal experience of the "inner witness of the Holy Spirit" before he could accept the Scriptures as being the Word of God and be converted. He writes this in his *Institutes:*

> Just as God alone is a fitting witness concerning Himself in His utterance, so also rthe utterance will not find faith in the hearts of men before it is sealed by the inner witness of the Spirit. The same Spirit, therefore, who spoke by the mouth of the prophets, must of necessity penetrate our hearts to persuade us that what was divinely commanded has been faithfully published (1,7,4).

> The Word itself is not fully certain to us unless confirmed by the witness of the Spirit . . . God sent the same Spirit, by whose virtue He had administered the Word, to complete His own work by the effective confirmation of the Word (1,9,3).

The Achilles heel of Calvin's "inner witness of the Holy Spirit" was that it made a *subjective* experience the basis for guaranteeing an *objective* revelation. The whole basis of faith was made to be dependent upon an inward subjective experience. This experience was thought to be the work of the Holy Spirit.

Calvin's teaching was the source of experiential religion on the American frontier during the nineteenth century. Coming to a "mourners bench" seeking the Holy Spirit, being "under conviction" and trying to "pray through" and experiencing "spiritual exercises" like fainting, barking and speaking in tongues were all thought to be a part of the Holy Spirit's work in conversion.

The experiential view of the Holy Spirit is found in what can be loosely called "Neo Orthodoxy."[8] This theological view, which permeates every brand of Protestant religion in Europe and America, has a philosophical basis in "existentialism." It regards truth as relative and impossible to discover in the absolute. There is no objective standard outside of oneself by which a person can judge anything. Truth is individualistic and is valid only as it is perceived. Someone can know only "his own truth," which might be contradictory to "other truth." The Scriptures are not verbally inspired, but only as they speak authentically to each individual. The relativism of new morality and situation ethics is an outgrowth of this thinking. The charismatic religions find their basis in this point of view.

We cannot remove the Holy Spirit from conversion any more than we can remove the vitality of a seed from the generation of a new plant.

Everything is based on the individual's experiential feelings when he comes to the "end of his rope" and leaps into the unknown. At this existential moment he experiences his own truth, which becomes the basis of his religious orientation. This is his "own truth" and his alone. It may be different from others' and contrary to reason and Scriptures. This makes no difference since Scriptures are human, truth is relative and man's own personal experience is the criteria for his faith. With this point of view everyone does what is right in his own eyes, and chaos ensues.

Conversion Influence Beyond the Word

The "Word only" view of the Holy Spirit's work in conversion also has problems. This view probably arose in opposition to the experiential view of the Holy Spirit.

It has much to commend it. It removes the religious authority of subjective experiences and replaces it with the objective standard of the Scriptures themselves. It affirms the pattern of New Testament conversions in which "faith came by hearing the Word of God." It disallows the speculations of men who would try to "add to" and "take away from" what God has revealed in the Scriptures. There are, however, two problems with this view.

First, it does not allow for the providence of God.[9] There is no question but that the "Word alone" is the source of faith. It is the only seed of the kingdom through which we can come to Christ. There is no question but that the "Word alone" is the means by which we can know the will of God, which we must obey to become a Christian. The Scriptures are all-sufficient. But can we say that God has nothing to do with getting the sinful man and the inspired message together through His providence?

Onesimus was the rebellious runaway slave. Philemon was his master. Somehow Onesimus, a lost sinner, came into contact with Paul while he was in prison at Rome. He heard the gospel and became a Christian. Paul sent him back to Philemon with a letter encouraging Philemon to receive him as a brother. In the letter Paul inferred that, perhaps, the providence of God played a part in all that had taken place: "For perhaps he was for this reason

Alive in the Spirit!

parted from you for a while, that you should have him back forever; no longer as a slave, but more than a slave, a beloved brother" (Philemon 15,16). Certainly, Paul was not suggesting any kind of miraculous activity of God in the conversion of Onesimus. He did not infer any kind of influence by the Holy Spirit in overpowering the will of man. This passage does suggest, however, that perhaps the providence of God can work to bring a man with a receptive heart into contact with one who will teach him the Gospel.

We must be careful in claiming the providence of God in any situation. Most things happen strictly as the result of natural causes. Certainly, the sovereign will of man cannot be ignored. We do not want to attribute something to the providence of God when that is not the case. Too often this is done as an excuse for not accepting responsibility or in explaining a tragic event. God does work in the world in a providential way, but man is not to be so presumptuous as to think he knows how and when He does.

Paul used what might be called the "providential perhaps" in speaking of the possibility of God working the life of Onesimus to bring about his conversion. It was "perhaps he departed" from you, not "hallelujah, praise God who made Onesimus run away." We must be careful in saying what God has done in providence.

Second, this view does not allow for the possibility of someone being converted through the influence of a Christian life, as well as instruction from the written Word.

There are times when a person's mind is so set that it cannot be changed by reason. His heart is so hardened that he rejects the written and spoken message of the Gospel. God can work in another way to change his heart. It is through the godly life of a Christian. This is particularly shown in the domestic relationship of a husband and wife.

> In the same way, you wives, be submissive to your own husbands so that even if any of them are disobedient to the word they may be won without a

His Work in Conversion

word by the behavior of their wives, as they observe your chaste and respectful behavior (1 Peter 3:1,2).

In this passage Peter showed that the "lived Word" is sometimes more powerful in conversion than the "spoken Word." The Holy Spirit not only works through the written Word of God to break and change the heart of a sinner. He also works in the godly life of a Christian to bring about conversion.

The "lived Word" cannot bring about conversion in and of itself. One cannot know the Gospel unless it is preached. Faith comes by hearing the Word of God. The seed of the Kingdom is the Word of God. God's will is revealed in words (1 Corinthians 2:13). The "lived Word," however, does influence people to be receptive to the "written Word." The Holy Spirit can work in both to bring about conversion.

Study Questions

1. Explain the Calvinistic term of the "inner witness" of the Holy Spirit.
2. What part does emotion play in conversion? Can emotions be trusted as a criteria for truth?
3. What part does the Holy Spirit play in conversion?
4. What is the philosophical and theological source of "relativism" in truth? Is it possible for there to be "my truth" and "your truth"?
5. Can someone be converted without the Word of God? Discuss.
6. Name two ways the Holy Spirit might work beyond the Word of God in conversion.
7. Assign someone who has a background in a better-felt-than-told religion to explain how and why he came out of it.
8. Memory work: John 3:5.

End Notes

[1]It is not the purpose of this book to be a polemic against the errors of Calvinism but to affirm the real work of the Holy Spirit in conversion. For a concise refutation of the "direct operation" of the Holy Spirit in conversion, see J. J. Turner and Edward P. Myers, *Doctrine of the Godhead* (West Monroe: Let the Bible Speak, Inc., 1973), pp. 113-115.

[2]Within the Restoration Movement were both extreme views of the work of the Holy Spirit in conversion. Alexander Campbell, following

Alive in the Spirit!

John Locke's theory of knowledge, defended the exclusive agency of the Word of God in conversion. Jesse B. Ferguson in Nashville and W. S. Russell in Illinois held to the "direct operation of the Holy Spirit" in conversion. Tolbert Fanning became the most outspoken advocate of the view that the Holy Spirit can work in the world only through the Word of God. Robert Richardson, though denying the work of the Holy Spirit in conversion, advocated that the Holy Spirit did personally dwell in the child of God. See Pat Brooks, "Robert Richardson: Nineteenth Century Advocate of Spirituality," *Restoration Quarterly*, XXI, 3, 1978, pp. 135-149, for a fuller discussion.

[3]See also James 1:18; 1 Peter 1:3; 1 John 5:18.

[4]God works through His preached Word to open the hearts of those who are lost. That was the case in the conversion of Lydia. Luke records that after Paul spoke the Word of the Lord that "the Lord opened her heart" (see Acts 16:14).

[5]The word translated "by" is *en*. It can also be translated "in" or "with." It is so translated in all of the passages involving baptism with *(en)* the Holy Spirit.

[6]See also 2 Corinthians 1:22; Romans 8:23.

[7]What is generally identified as gnosticism came about later. The roots of gnosticism are already to be seen in the New Testament.

[8]The term "neo orthodoxy" can be defined as a movement in contemporary theology that emphasizes the classical Protestant doctrine of God's transcendence, man's sin and justification by faith and at the same time denying the inspiration of the Scriptures.

[9]Providence is used here not in its Calvinistic sense but as nonmiraculous workings of God in the world for the benefit of man.

ELEVEN

His Work Through the Word

There is no question but that the Holy Spirit works through the Word of God. The Holy Spirit is the agent, and the Word is an instrument which the agent uses.

Numerous New Testament passages show the Holy Spirit as the source and the Word of God as an instrument in accomplishing His work in the world. The Holy Spirit reveals God's will through the Word of God (2 Peter 1:20,21). The Holy Spirit convicts the world of sin, righteousness and judgment through the Word of God (John 16:8). The Holy Spirit guided the apostles into all truth through the Word of God (John 16:13).

This is to be compared to Jesus working through His Word in judgment. He warned those who rejected Him that His Word would judge them: "He who rejects Me, and does not receive My sayings, has one who judges him, the word I spoke is what will judge him at the last day" (John 12:48). Jesus and His words are not the same, but to reject His person is to be judged by His words. One is the agent, and the other is an instrument of the agent.

Many of the things that the Scriptures say that the Holy Spirit does, they also say are done by the Word of God. This should present no problem. Such language is currently used in daily activities.

You could say, for instance, that the words I am now writing were written by the word processor, if you were speaking of the *instrument* of writing. You could also say that the same words were written by Jimmy Jividen, if you were speaking of the *agent* of the writing. This use of language is found in speaking of the Holy Spirit and the Word of God. One is the *agent*, and the other is an *instrument* the agent uses to do His work in the world. This is shown in the following chart.

Action	Holy Spirit	Word of God
Creation	Genesis 1:2; Job 33:4	Hebrews 1:3
Power	Romans 15:13	Luke 1:37
Truth	John 16:13	John 17:17
Bear Witness	John 15:26	John 20:30-31
Birth	John 3:5-8	1 Peter 1:23
Salvation	Titus 3:5	James 1:21
Dwells in	Romans 8:11	Colossians 3:16
Comforts	Acts 9:31	Romans 15:4
Sanctifies	2 Thessalonians 2:13	John 17:17

Some people have confused the Holy Spirit with one of the instruments He uses to work in the world.

The present work of the Holy Spirit is easiest to identify as He works through the Word of God for four reasons.

First, all one can know about The Holy Spirit is through the Word of God. There is no other way to know about either His person or His work. The attempts of men to identify the Holy Spirit with warm emotional feelings or paranormal events in nature are deceitful. Pagans have the same kinds of feelings and do the same kinds of things and claim that their gods are working in them. John gave a warning to those who would be led astray by such claims: "Beloved, do not believe every spirit, but test the spirits to see whether they are from God; because many false prophets have gone out into the world" (1 John 4:1). There are *unholy* spirits as well as the *Holy* Spirit. What some think to be the Holy Spirit are, in reality, false claims from false prophets.

His Work Through the Word

Second, the Holy Spirit is the "inspirer" of the Word of God. This relationship makes it easier to understand His working through the Word. Peter clearly states the work of the Holy Spirit in producing Scriptures: "But know this first of all, that no prophecy of Scripture is a matter of one's own interpretation, for no prophecy was ever made by an act of human will, but men moved by the Holy Spirit spoke from God" (2 Peter 1:20,21). Scriptures did not come from the theological speculation of the prophets and apostles; they came from God. Men and their language were only instruments that the Holy Spirit used to communicate God's will.

Certainly there are ways the Spirit and the Word of Christ can be related, but the language of the texts does not show them to be identical. If the Holy Spirit wanted to show that, He had adequate language to express it.

This was understood by the writers of the New Testament. The writer of Hebrews twice quoted from the same Old Testament passage (Hebrews 3:7,8; 4:7). The first time he attributed it to the Holy Spirit. The second time he attributed it to David. He was correct both times. The first time he spoke of the spiritual source, the Holy Spirit. The second time he spoke of the human agent, David. The Scriptures cannot be separated from their source. The Holy Spirit inspired the men who wrote them. They are "God breathed."[1]

Third, the Holy Spirit is easier to understand through the written word because it is physical and visible. We can see, hear and feel the Word of God. That cannot be done with the work of the Holy Spirit when He intercedes for the Christian in his prayers. That is known only by faith.

It is more difficult to understand things in the realm of faith than things in the physical realm. God understood this limitation of man. So, to reveal Himself, He became flesh. He broke into the physical realm with His only begotten Son. The incarnation was God's attempt to make Himself known. Numerous passages express this truth.

> And the Word became flesh, and dwelt among us, and we beheld His glory, glory as of the only begotten from the Father, full of grace and truth (John 1:14).
>
> "If you had known Me, you would have known My Father also; from now on you know Him, and have seen Him." Philip said to Him, "Lord, show us the Father, and it is enough for us." Jesus said to him, "Have I been so long with you, and yet you have not come to know Me, Philip? He who has seen Me has seen the Father" (John 14:7-9).

We can better know God because Jesus, as flesh and blood, revealed God in the physical realm. We can better know the Holy Spirit because of the Word of God which exists in the physical realm.

Fourth, many things done by the Holy Spirit are also done by the Word of God, as seen in the previous chart.

The work of the Holy Spirit through the Word of God might be easier for us to understand, but this does not negate His other work in a realm that we can only know by faith.

The Worker and His Work

The Holy Spirit is the worker, and the Word of God is His work. They must not be confused. The Word of God is only one of the works of the Holy Spirit. The opposite is not true. The Holy Spirit is the only source of the Word of God. The Holy Spirit and the Word of God are not the same. The Word of God cannot be separated from the

Holy Spirit, but the Holy Spirit can be separated from the Word of God.

Jesus *worked* miracles, but that fact did not make *Jesus* a miracle. That fact did not demand that Jesus work *only* through miracles. Jesus was the worker; the miracles were the works He did. They were not the same.

It is true that a person and his words are related. They are not, however, related on a level plain. The man is the source of his words, and his words cannot exist without him. This is not true from the other side. Though a man's word cannot exist without him, the man can exist without his words and function in many other ways. The man is the worker, a person. The words are his work, a thing.

Both Spirit and Word

The distinction between the Holy Spirit and the Word of God is shown in the Scriptures themselves. Both the Holy Spirit and the Word of God are used in the same context to mean different things. This would be redundant if the only way the Holy Spirit worked in the world was through the Word of God.

> . . . for our gospel did not come to you in word only, but also in power and in the Holy Spirit and with full conviction (1 Thessalonians 1:5).

> For in the case of those who have once been enlightened and have tasted of the heavenly gift and have been made partakers of the Holy Spirit, and have tasted the good word of God and the powers of the age to come, and then have fallen away, it is impossible to renew them again to repentance (Hebrews 6:4-6).

It is clear in these passages that the Word of God is different from the Holy Spirit.

This distinction is also evident in the armor analogy Paul used in writing to the church at Ephesus: "And take the helmet of salvation and the sword of the Spirit, which is the word of God" (Ephesians 6:17). The Word of God is as different from the Holy Spirit as a sword is from the soldier who uses it. There are other parts of the armor besides the sword and other functions of the soldier besides wielding the sword. Even so, there are other instruments of the Holy Spirit besides the Word of God and other functions of the Holy Spirit besides what He does through the Word of God. The soldier and the sword are not the same, nor are the Holy Spirit and the Word of God the same.

The distinction between the Holy Spirit and the Word of God is shown in the language Luke used for the conversion of the Samaritans. The Samaritan "received the Word of God" when Philip preached to them (Acts 8:14). They were baptized. Receiving the Word of God was not the same as receiving the Holy Spirit, for Luke later recorded that the Holy Spirit "had not yet fallen upon any of them" (Acts 8:16).[2] The Holy Spirit and the Word of God are not the same.

Ephesians 5:18,19 and Colossians 3:16

Two similar passages from Paul's prison epistles are sometimes understood to teach that the Word of God and the Holy Spirit are inseparable. One passage admonishes Christians to be "filled with the Spirit," and the other passage encourages Christians to "let the word of Christ richly dwell within you." These passages are similar in other ways; so, it is thought that the Word of God and the Spirit should be equated. It might be helpful to examine the passages in two columns.

Ephesians 5:18-19	**Colossians 3:16**
but be filled with the Spirit	*Let the word of Christ dwell within you*
speaking to one another in psalms and hymns and spiritual songs	with all wisdom teaching and admonishing one another with psalms and hymns and spiritual songs
singing and making melody with your heart to the Lord	singing with thanksgiving in your hearts to God.

His Work Through the Word

It can be seen that the two passages are similar in some of the wording, but they are not so similar in their context. The Ephesian passage is in the literary context of describing the Christian walk and prohibits getting drunk with wine. The Colossian passage is in the literary context of "putting on" the new self which involved letting (1) the peace of Christ rule in your hearts (2) the Word of Christ dwell within you and (3) whatever you do in word or deed, do all in the name of the Lord Jesus. The emphasis is on living a renewed life reflecting the "new self."

Neither passage is talking about how the Holy Spirit dwells in a Christian but about how to sing. The use of "Spirit" in one passage and "word of Christ" in the other

---

The Holy Spirit is the worker, and the Word of God is His work. They must not be confused. The Word of God is only one of the works of the Holy Spirit. The Word of God cannot be separated from the Holy Spirit, but the Holy Spirit can be separated from the Word of God.

---

passage no more proves that the Spirit dwells in the Christian through the Word than does a soldier and a sword being in the same house prove that the soldier dwells in the house through the sword. Certainly there are ways the Spirit and the Word of Christ can be related, but the language of the texts does not show them to be identical. If the Holy Spirit wanted to show that, He had adequate language to express it.

It should be noted that both the indwelling of the "Word of Christ" and being "filled with the Spirit" were ex-

Alive in the Spirit!

pressed by words. In Ephesians it is under the expression of "speaking." In Colossians it is under the expression of "teaching." This shows the close relationship between being "filled with the Spirit" and having the "word of Christ" dwelling in a person.

The phrase "filled with the Spirit" is used at least nine times in the New Testament.[3] If this expression means being "filled with the Word of God" in Ephesians 5:18, then it must mean being "filled with the Word of God" in the other passages also. Does such an interpretation fit?

It is true that seven of these nine passages connect speaking with being "filled with the Spirit."[4] The context of each of these passages could well be that what was spoken was the "Word of God." Both Zacharias and Elizabeth spoke prophetically about Jesus' birth (Luke 1:41,67). The apostles spoke the "Word of God" in other languages on Pentecost (Acts 2:4). After being "filled with the Spirit," Luke records that a whole group "began to speak the word of God with boldness" (Acts 4:31).

Two of the nine passages do not connect being "filled with the Spirit" with the "Word of God" (Luke 1:15; Acts 9:17). There is nothing said about the "Word of God" when the angel predicted that John the Baptist would be "filled with the Holy Spirit" while yet in his mother's womb (Luke 1:15). When Ananias laid his hands on Saul in Damascus and promised that he would regain his sight and be filled with the Holy Spirit, he was not talking about Saul being "filled with the word of God" (Acts 9:17).

The admonition that Paul gave to the church at Ephesus to "be filled with the Spirit" could include being filled with "the Word of God." It could also refer to other kinds of functions of the Holy Spirit.

When we try to discover the metaphysics of "how" the Holy Spirit dwells in a Christian, the Scriptures do not give much information. They affirm *that* the Holy Spirit dwells in a Christian, but not *how*.

There has been a lot of discussion about the "mode" of indwelling of the Holy Spirit. Does He dwell in a Christian literally, personally, figuratively, representatively

His Work Through the Word

or some other way? The discussion has centered on theological speculation rather than divine revelation. The Scriptures just do not reveal the "mode" of indwelling of the Holy Spirit. Furman Kearley has made a very clear statement of this fact in *God's Indwelling Spirit* (Montgomery: Bible & School Supply, 1974):

> The brethren who believe in representative indwelling by means of the word often criticize those holding the view of the actual indwelling of the Holy Spirit because they say the Holy Spirit dwells in Christians "personally." They contend the scriptures nowhere use the word "personally." I would respond by saying "Show me the verse that says 'representatively,' and I will show the verse that says 'personally'."
>
> We do not understand how the human spirit dwells in us, but we accept it. Even so, we may not comprehend how the Holy Spirit dwells in us, but we must accept that He does.

We cannot even know all about how the Word of God dwells in a person. It's certainly not literally, unless we would eat a Bible. It's certainly not personally, since the Word of God is not a person. Is it by thoughts? Is it by will? Is it through influence? There is no word from the Lord on this, so we must be silent.

In the first few centuries of our era, Christians had many controversies over *how* God became flesh in Jesus Christ. They got so involved in the metaphysical questions of *how* Jesus became flesh that many of them lost sight of the Scriptural affirmation that He *did* become flesh.

There are two problems about understanding the work of the Holy Spirit in the Christian. First, some people try to "figure out" things the Scriptures do not reveal. Second, some people try to "feel out" things the Scriptures do not reveal. Both are wrong. It is just as wrong to "go beyond" the teachings of Christ by straining a passage to make it say what we desire as it is to "go beyond" the teachings of Christ to listen to a delusion from one's own emotional experience.

What is the evidence for the indwelling of the Holy Spirit? Can He dwell in a person without his being aware of it? Can a person receive the Holy Spirit at baptism and live the Christian life for years without knowing that the Holy Spirit dwells in him?

We must understand that the Holy Spirit does not take up space, and neither can He be measured by weight. He is Spirit. He exists in another realm that is different from the material world in which man lives. We are not promised nor must we expect some kind of physical manifestation of the Holy Spirit's presence.

---

*There are **unholy** spirits as well as the **Holy** Spirit. What some think to be the Holy Spirit are, in reality, false claims from false prophets.*

A baby does not know that he possesses the genes of his parents when he is born. The fact that a child possesses the genes of his parents is not known by most people of the world. This lack of knowledge or discernible evidence, however, does not mean that a child does not have his parents' genes.

There are two ways that a Christian can know that the Holy Spirit dwells in him. The first is by the promise of the Scriptures.[5] The other is by the fruit of the Spirit that is manifested in his life.[6]

A groom waits in expectation for his bride to come down the aisle. Finally, the father of the bride enters carrying a package. When the preacher asks, "Who gives this bride?" the father of the bride hands the groom a tape recording of the voice of the bride. The groom is disappointed. He had been promised a person, but he has only been given her words. The father of the bride explains to the groom that he is giving his daughter to him only through the medium of her words. The groom remains unconvinced and disappointed. You cannot substitute a thing for a person.

We cannot know all about how the Word of God dwells in a person. It's certainly not literally, unless we would eat a Bible. It's certainly not personally, since the Word of God is not a person. Is it by thoughts? Is it by will? Is it through influence? There is no word from the Lord on this, so we must be silent.

Study Questions

1. List nine ways in which the Scriptures say that something is done by both the Holy Spirit and the Word of God.
2. Describe the relationship that the Holy Spirit has to the Word of God.
3. Discuss the difference between "being filled with the Spirit" and letting the "Word of Christ dwell within you" as found in Ephesians 5:18 and Colossians 3:16.
4. Can we know *how* the Holy Spirit dwells in a child of God? Discuss.
5. How can we know that the Holy Spirit dwells in him?
6. What is the "fruit of the Spirit" in Galatians 5:22,23?
7. What is the only means by which we can know of the nature and the work of the Holy Spirit?
8. Memory work: Ephesians 6:17.

Alive in the Spirit!

End Notes

[1] The word, *theopneustos*, translated "inspired by God" in 2 Timothy 3:16 literally means, "God-breathed."

[2] The context shows that this reception of the Holy Spirit involved the laying on of the apostles' hands which was different from the gift of the Holy Spirit which they received at baptism.

[3] Luke 1:15,41,67; Acts 2:4; 4:8,31; 9:17; 13:9; Ephesians 3:19.

[4] Luke 1:41,67; Acts 2:4; 4:8; 4:31; Ephesians 3:19.

[5] Acts 2:38. The promise of the "gift of the Holy Spirit" is given on the same basis as the promise of the "forgiveness of sins." They are both true because they are promised by inspiration.

[6] Galatians 5:22,23. The fruit of the Spirit expresses the Christian's attitude or demeanor. A more important question than "How does the Holy Spirit dwell in a Christian?" is the practical question of "Why is there so little evidence that the Holy Spirit dwells in a Christian?"

TWELVE

His Work in the Christian

The language that Jesus used to promise the Holy Spirit to His disciples is applicable, in some ways, for Christians in every generation: "And I will ask the Father, and He will give you another Helper, that He may be with you forever; that is the Spirit of truth, whom the world cannot receive . . . I will not leave you as orphans" (John 14:16-18). The Holy Spirit is the Helper that every Christian in every age receives at baptism. Certainly, the Holy Spirit does not work in the same miraculous way as He did in those Christians of the apostolic community, but He is still the Helper. God has not left the Christian alone in the world.

It has already been shown in Chapter 5 that the "gift of the Holy Spirit" is given to all of God's children. He dwells in the Christian as a heavenly guest. It is through the Holy Spirit that the Christian finds his identity as God's child and as a brother or sister to the rest of God's family. The Holy Spirit is the Helper. But how does He help?

Certainly, the Holy Spirit helps the Christian through the Word of God. By His work in the Scriptures, we can know God's will. We can be inspired and motivated by the Gospel story. We can obtain the knowledge and understanding necessary to grow to spiritual maturity. We can know the basis and results of divine judgment. But is that all? Does the Holy Spirit work through the Word of God only?

Certainly not. There is a difference in saying that the Holy Spirit works through the Word of God and in saying

Alive in the Spirit!

it's the *only* way He works. We can say that a man is saved by faith. That is true. If we say, however, that a man is saved by faith *alone*, we would be wrong. We can truly say that a man is saved by grace. It is wrong, however, to say that a man is saved by grace *alone*. We can truly say that the Holy Spirit works through the Word. It would be wrong to say that the Holy Spirit works through the Word *alone*.

The Jew before Christ had the Word of God in the Scriptures of the Old Testament. The Christian has more than the Jew. A Christian not only has the Word of God in the Scriptures, but he also has the Holy Spirit dwelling in him. This might be called the "Christian advantage."

Beyond What We Think

The indwelling of the Holy Spirit has already been shown. The next question, "What does He do today?"

He does not work in a miraculous way today. There is no such promise. There is no such need. There is no such evidence. This would be contrary to the orderliness of God in both creation and revelation.[1]

He does not work by human emotional experiences. Such emotional experiences are common to the human situation, especially in a religious context. There is no evidence in the New Testament that such experiences were a part of the work of the Holy Spirit.

He does work in a real and orderly way. This is the promise of the Scriptures. Paul prayed for the Holy Spirit to work in the lives of the Christians at Ephesus.

> . . . that He would grant you, according to the riches of His glory, to be strengthened with power through His Spirit in the inner man; so that Christ may dwell in your hearts through faith . . . Now to Him who is able to do exceeding abundantly beyond all that we ask or think, according to the power that works within us, to Him be the glory in the church and in Christ Jesus to all generations forever and ever (Ephesians 3:16,17, 20,21).

This prayer is for all of the church, not just a few who had special powers from the Holy Spirit. Paul prayed that they might be strengthened with power through the Spirit. This power was within them. God can work through this power to do more than we can possibly ask or think.

This passage shows that God's work through His Spirit in the inner man is greater than our words can speak or our minds can think. This certainly suggests that the work of the Holy Spirit cannot be limited to a group of theological statements someone might set down. There are ways in which the Scriptures affirm that the Holy Spirit works in the world. These ways cannot be denied. There are also ways that He works beyond the realm of this material world and beyond the limitations of language. We can say nothing about these things because even God is silent about them.

There are at least five ways in which the Holy Spirit works beyond the Word of God today.

Assurance

First, the indwelling of the Holy Spirit gives assurance to us as Christians that we are God's children. The connecting link that Christians have with God is the Holy Spirit. This is the affirmation of Paul:

> And because you are sons, God has sent forth the Spirit of His Son into your hearts, crying, "Abba! Father!" (Galatians 4:6).

> For all who are being led by the Spirit of God, these are sons of God. For you have not received a spirit of slavery leading to fear again, but you have received a spirit of adoption as sons by which we cry out, "Abba! Father!" The Spirit Himself bears witness with our spirit that we are children of God (Romans 8:14-16).

The Holy Spirit is the connecting link of our relationship with God. We can call God, "Abba! Father!" because we are identified as God's children by the Holy Spirit.

Alive in the Spirit!

We Christians do not have to wallow in the mire of despair and doubt, wondering if we are accepted as God's son. We are not stepsons, sons-in-law or duty-driven slaves. We are children begotten by the Father, born of the water and the Spirit and have received the mark of sonship, the Holy Spirit. We do not have to have self-doubts of our relationship with God. God has acknowledged us as His sons. We have blessed assurance. We are confident of our salvation and assured that we have a Father who loves us, hears us and cares about our every need.

The Scriptures affirm that the Holy Spirit bears witness with our spirits. Some people in both the first century and the 20th century have suggested that this is the direct operation of God in some kind of intuitive, experiential way. This is wrong. It is not what you feel. It is not an experiential claim to the indwelling of God without regard to what you believe, what you practice or how you obey the commands of the Scriptures. John refuted those who held this false faith. Knowing God is determined by what you believe (1 John 4:1-3; 2 John 7-9). Knowing God is determined by how you obey His commandments (1 John 5:2,3; John 14:15). Knowing God is determined by how you practice brotherly love (1 John 3:14-19). Two passages in First John refute the idea that the Holy Spirit works in an experiential way.

> And by this we know that we have come to know Him, if we keep His commandments. The one who says, "I have come to know Him," and does not keep His commandments, is a liar and the truth is not in him; but whoever keeps His word, in Him the love of God has truly been perfected, By this we know that we are in Him (1 John 2:3-5).

> And the one who keeps His commandments abides in Him, and He in him. And we know by this that He abides in us, by the Spirit which He has given us (1 John 3:24).

His Work in the Christian

The basis of our assurance of being children of God is not subjective emotionalism. It is rather the objective criteria of keeping the commandments of the Lord. When this is done, the Holy Spirit bears witness with the spirit of man.

Moral Help

Second, the indwelling of the Holy Spirit helps us to live moral, godly lives. It takes more than the written Word of God and the strong will of man to live a life of holiness. True holiness is only possible because of the help that God gives through the Holy Spirit.

The Jews before Christ had the written Word of God. It revealed the will of God and pronounced judgment on those who disobeyed it. They did not keep the Word of God. The Word of God, therefore, became to them the means through which they knew of their sin (Romans 2:12,13; 3:23).

Christians also have the Word of God. We have two things the Jews did not have. We have forgiveness of sins through the atoning sacrifice of Jesus Christ. We have the help of God in overcoming sin through the indwelling of the Holy Spirit.

Because of the indwelling of the Holy Spirit, Christians have a higher motive to refrain from sin. Paul taught the Corinthians to abstain from fornication because of the indwelling Holy Spirit. The Christian's body is the dwelling place of the Holy Spirit and should not be defiled with immorality.

> Flee immorality. Every other sin that a man commits is outside the body, but the immoral man sins against his own body. Or do you not know that your body is the temple of the Holy Spirit who is in you, whom you have from God, and that you are not your own? (1 Corinthians 6:18,19).[2]

Immorality is more than just a social sin against another human being. It is a sin against God. It defiles the very holiness of God's temple, the Christian's physical body.

Alive in the Spirit!

Paul recognized the great paradox found in every Christian's life. His will is pulled in two directions—between good and evil. In this internal tug-of-war, man finds himself a wretched, miserable creature: "For the good that I wish, I do not do; but I practice the very evil that I do not wish . . . Wretched man that I am! Who will set me free from the body of this death? Thanks be to God through Jesus Christ our Lord" (Romans 7:19,24,25). The internal tug-of-war within man between the noble desire for good and the actual practice of evil has been overcome by the help of God. This help involves both the sacrifice of Jesus and the indwelling of the Holy Spirit.

In the same letter Paul taught that the Holy Spirit helps us live the Christian life. Christians have an advantage. The Holy Spirit *dwells* in us. We *mind* the things of the Spirit; we *walk* after the Spirit; we receive life by the Spirit; we are *led* by the Spirit; by the Spirit we *put to death* the deeds of the body (see Romans 8).

The advantage Christians have over the Jews is that we have the indwelling of the Holy Spirit. God gives Christians greater grace than He did the Jews.

God has promised help to Christians in overcoming temptation. We cannot always know how God does this. We certainly must not set human limitations on the workings of God. The help of the Holy Spirit might be involved. He is called the "Helper."[3] God's promise of help is clear:

> No temptation has overtaken you but such as is common to man; and God is faithful, who will not allow you to be tempted beyond what you are able; but with the temptation will provide the way of escape also, that you may be able to endure it (1 Corinthians 10:13).

There will always be a "way of escape" for Christians who are tempted. God has promised a way of escape and the strength to overcome the temptation. Perhaps part of this help comes from the power of the Holy Spirit in the inner man which is described as being greater than we can possibly ask or think (Ephesians 3:16-20).

By the grace of God, the example of Jesus and the help of the Holy Spirit Christians can overcome temptation.

Providence

Third, the indwelling of the Holy Spirit works in providence. It was in the context of the work of the Holy Spirit that Paul affirmed the purposeful activity of God which helps Christians in this world.

> And we know that God causes all things to work together for good to those who love God, to those who are called according to His purpose . . . What then shall we say to these things? If God is for us, who is against us? He who did not spare His own Son, but delivered Him up for us all, how will He not also with Him freely give us all things (Romans 8:28,31,32).

God, in ways we cannot always understand, causes the events of the world to work together for the good of Christians. This non-miraculous, behind-the-scene working of God is promised to "those who love God and are called." This help involves "all things." The promise is affirmed even stronger through the statement Paul makes: "If God wanted to do good for His children enough to deliver up His own Son," He will surely freely give them all things they need.

The passage shows that God continues to work in the world in providence. This is different from either His work through the Word of God or His work through miracles. Certainly, He who spoke the worlds into existence and presently sustains them by the Word of His power is able to make nature, history, tragic events and even evil people work together to accomplish His purposes.

The promise of this kind of help from God comes in the context of the Holy Spirit's present work in the world.

The possibility of this kind of help from the Holy Spirit beyond the Word of God should present no theological problem. God works in us (Philippians 2:13). Christ enables Christians to do all things (Philippians 4:13). Surely the indwelling Spirit is able to work in providence for the Christian's good.

Worship

Fourth, the indwelling of the Holy Spirit aids Christians in worship. He is uniquely qualified to do so. Worship is *spiritual* communication with God. Jesus instructed the Samaritan woman about the spiritual nature of worship: "God is spirit and those who worship Him must worship in spirit and truth" (John 4:24).

How can man, who is physical, commune with God, who is spiritual? Man and God have different realms of existence. How can the barriers which divide these realms of existence be overcome?

Certainly, the mediation of Jesus helps. He who is God, a spiritual being, became man, a physical being. He is able to understand man and his plight because He Himself was flesh and blood: "For there is one God, and one mediator also between God and men, the man Christ Jesus, who gave Himself as a ransom for all" (1 Timothy 2:5,6).[4] Jesus' mediation aids us in coming to God in worship. He understands our human plight on earth and, yet, rules as God in heaven. He mediates between the spiritual and physical realms and bridges the communication gap between God and man.

The help of the Holy Spirit is also involved in worship. The Holy Spirit who knows the mind of God but dwells in man is able to help Christians as we seek to commune with God. Two passages help us to understand this.

> For who among men knows the thoughts of a man except the Spirit of the man, which is in him? Even so the thoughts of God no one knows except the Spirit of God (1 Corinthians 2:11).

His Work in the Christian

> And in the same way the Spirit also helps our weakness for we do not know how to pray as we should, but the Spirit Himself intercedes for us with groanings too deep for words; for He who searches the hearts knows what the mind of the Spirit is, because He intercedes for the saints according to the will of God (Romans 8:26,27).

The Holy Spirit helps the children of God in our prayers in ways that are not fully revealed. We can know that this help is not any kind of "prayer language" because it is "groanings too deep for words." Someway He who dwells in man and knows the thoughts of his spirit is able to intercede on his behalf before God. When we have yearnings too deep for words and are unable to verbalize all of our desires which we want to lay before God's throne of grace, the Holy Spirit is able to help our weaknesses. We can know that God knows about and understands what we want to express in praoyer.

We might not understand the metaphysics of how the Holy Spirit helps in prayer any more than we understand the metaphysics of how Jesus helps in intercession. We just believe it. It is in this faith that we have confidence in our devotion to God.

Fruit

Fifth, the indwelling of the Holy Spirit helps Christians in our attitudes. Attitudes do not come from a vacuum. They are willed by the person possessing them, and the Holy Spirit helps in exercising them. This seems to be the meaning of Paul's discussion of the fruit of the Spirit: "But the fruit of the Spirit is love, joy, peace, patience, kindness, goodness, faithfulness, gentleness, self control; against such there is no law" (Galatians 5:22,23). The nine attitude attributes listed in this passage are described as "fruit of the Spirit." This fruit is contrasted to the 15 "deeds of the flesh," which prohibit us from inheriting the kingdom of God. He then shows how we can overcome the desires of the flesh by walking after the Spirit: "But I say, walk by the Spirit, and you will not carry out the desire of the flesh" (Galatians 5:16). Walking by the Spirit causes us to possess the fruit of the Spirit. Again, the text does not indicate *how* the Spirit is involved. It could be "through the word of God inspired by the Holy Spirit." It could be "through the power that the Spirit gives in the inner man." It could be "through the help of the Spirit in prayer." It could be "through the providence of God which provided help in overcoming temptation."

These attitude attributes come from the Spirit who dwells in Christians. Their possession reflects the indwelling of the Holy Spirit in Christians. If Christians do not possess these attitude attributes we are "resisting the Spirit" (Ephesians 4:30) or "quenching the Spirit" (1 Thessalonians 5:19).

The Holy Spirit dwells in Christians. By the Spirit Christians find identity as God's children and a bond of brotherhood in the church. By the Spirit we have power beyond what can be spoken or thought. By the Spirit we have help in worship and strength to overcome temptation. The Holy Spirit continues His work in the world. He works through the Word of God. He works in the church. He works in every Christian. We who have received the gift of the Holy Spirit are indeed blessed. We have the divine Helper.

Study Questions

1. Does God still work in the world today? Does Christ still control the affairs of men? Does the Holy Spirit still help Christians? Discuss.
2. Explain how the "power of the inner man" is able to do exceeding abundantly beyond all that we ask or think. See Ephesians 3:16-20.
3. How does the Holy Spirit help us to know we are children of God?
4. How does the Holy Spirit help us live godly lives?
5. How does the Holy Spirit help us in prayer?
6. Can we know *that* God works in providence? Can we know *how* God works in providence?

His Work in the Christian

7. Discuss how the Holy Spirit works in an orderly way according to God's laws in nature and in revelation.
8. Memory work: 1 John 3:24.

End Notes

[1] See Jimmy Jividen, *Miracles, From God or Man?* (Abilene: ACU Press, 1988).

[2] See also 1 Thessalonians 4:3-8.

[3] The word translated "Helper" is *paracletos*. It means "one called along side to help." This term is used of the Holy Spirit in John 14:16,26; 15:26; 16:7.

[4] See also Hebrews 7:25 and 1 John 2:1.